Choosing **TRUE** Happiness

Choosing **TRUE** Happiness

BE HAPPY NOW

MICHAEL C. YENZER

Copyrighted Material

Choosing True Happiness: Be Happy Now

Copyright © 2022 by Michael C. Yenzer. All Rights Reserved.

No part of this publication may be reproduced, stored in a retrieval system or transmitted, in any form or by any means—electronic, mechanical, photocopying, recording or otherwise—without prior written permission from the publisher, except for the inclusion of brief quotations in a review.

For information about this title or to order other books and/or electronic media, contact the publisher:

Michael C. Yenzer
choosingtruehappiness.com
choosing.truehappiness@gmail.com

ISBNs:
978-1-7366656-0-2 (softcover)
978-1-7366656-1-9 (eBook)

Printed in the United States of America

Cover and Interior design: 1106 Design

Although the author has made every effort to ensure that the information in this book was correct at press time and while this publication is designed to provide accurate information in regard to the subject matter covered, the author assumes no responsibility for errors, inaccuracies, omissions, or any other inconsistencies herein and hereby disclaim any liability to any party for any loss, damage, or disruption caused by errors or omissions, whether such errors or omissions result from negligence, accident, or any other cause.

This publication is meant as a source of valuable information for the reader, however it is not meant as a substitute for direct expert assistance. If such level of assistance is required, the services of a competent professional should be sought.

The author is providing this book and its contents on an "as is" basis and makes no representations or warranties of any kind with respect to this book or its contents. The author disclaims all such representations and warranties, including but not limited to warranties of healthcare for a particular purpose.

The author makes no guarantees concerning the level of success you may experience by following the advice and strategies contained in this book, and you accept the risk that results will differ for each individual. The testimonials and examples provided in this book show exceptional results, which may not apply to the average reader, and are not intended to represent or guarantee that you will achieve the same or similar results.

The content of this book is for informational purposes only and is not intended to diagnose, treat, cure, or prevent any condition or disease. You understand that this book is not intended as a substitute for consultation with a licensed practitioner. Please consult with your own physician or healthcare specialist regarding the suggestions and recommendations made in this book. You are responsible for your own choices, actions, and results. The use of this book implies your acceptance of this disclaimer.

Why did I choose to write a self-help book?

Here are some of the reasons:

* To pay it forward and help others conquer depression and anxiety. I wanted people to know if I can beat depression and anxiety, so can they. Depression and anxiety are treatable and beatable illnesses.
* To help people who struggle with addictions
* To share how I achieved true happiness with the rest of the world. The world needs happier people. It's my great hope that many people will benefit from purchasing this book and live a truly happy life.
* To raise awareness for people to realize that we are all part of one family, God's Family.
* To help you grow spiritually and find your own God zone.
* To encourage and help people to believe, trust, and have faith in God and have a relationship with God.
* To help people manage their thoughts, emotions, and actions.
* To help spread love and positive energy—the world can really use it.
* To help all people increase their happiness level and be happy most of the time.
* To encourage you to use positive coping skills, be mentally strong, and improve your mental health.
* To improve the quality of your life, regardless of what challenges you are facing.
* To teach that getting help for yourself or others is a sign of honesty, intelligence, strength, and courage. Everybody needs help at some point in their life.
* To inspire people to be more courageous and never, ever give up, regardless of what challenges/struggles they are facing.

CHOOSING TRUE HAPPINESS

* To encourage people to treat one another with more love, respect, kindness, and compassion.
* To raise a lot of money for five amazing charities and to encourage other kind deeds.
* To leave my legacy for my two daughters.
* To create a valuable resource that will help many generations to come.
* To help people believe that there's always hope, help, and faith.
* To bring honor and glory to God and fulfill part of my purpose.

In loving memory of my nonno and nonna, whose support, influence, and love made this book possible.

Rapping Helps Heads

Soon you will see
What this mnemonic device can really be
It can provide you with much cheer
Just follow each letter, and be sure to adhere

Relationships: Make them really special and meaningful
Appreciation: Think it, feel it, and show it often
Perspective: Keep it positive, please
Positive Support System: Is one in place?
I agree—it's up to me. I am my own biggest project
Nutrition—you are what you eat
Good sense of humor—just laugh

Help often, and you shall receive
Exercise is the key—just do it
Love, Love, Love
Pray every day
Sleep well and rejuvenate

Hugs feel great
Express yourself in an appropriate and healthy manner
Attitude worth catching?
Dream on
Seek God, and grow spiritually

Table of Contents

Introduction (11)   xv

Chapter One:
Awareness and Being (14)   1

Chapter Two:
Relationships: Make Them Really Special and Meaningful (18)   5

Chapter Three:
Appreciation: Think It, Feel It, and Show It Often (26)   11

Chapter Four:
Perspective: Keep It Positive, Please (38)   19

Chapter Five:
Positive Support System: Is One in Place? (49)   27

Chapter Six:
I Agree—It's Up to Me. I Am My Own Biggest Project (55)   31

Chapter Seven:
Nutrition: You Are What You Eat (104)   57

CHOOSING TRUE HAPPINESS

Chapter Eight: Good Sense of Humor: Just Laugh (113)	63
Chapter Nine: Help Often, and You Shall Receive (121)	69
Chapter Ten: Exercise Is the Key: Just Do It (126)	73
Chapter Eleven: Love, Love, Love (130)	77
Chapter Twelve: Pray Every Day (138)	83
Chapter Thirteen: Sleep Well and Rejuvenate (143)	87
Chapter Fourteen: Hugs Feel Great (148)	91
Chapter Fifteen: Express Yourself in an Appropriate and Healthy Manner (153)	95
Chapter Sixteen: Attitude: Worth Catching? (166)	105
Chapter Seventeen: Dream On (179)	117
Chapter Eighteen: Seek God, and Grow Spiritually (184)	121
Chapter Nineteen: Happy: To Be or Not to Be? Choose Intelligently (192)	127

TABLE OF CONTENTS

Chapter Twenty:
The Most and the Greatest (254)   173

Chapter Twenty-One:
Daily Happiness Checklist (255)   175

Chapter Twenty-Two:
ABCs of Happiness (259)   177

Chapter Twenty-Three:
Positive Affirmations (260)   179

Chapter Twenty-Four
In a Nutshell (264)   183

Chapter Twenty-Five:
RAP Your Way to Happiness (266)   185

Chapter Twenty-Six:
TEA (267)   187

Chapter Twenty-Seven:
It All Starts With Your Thoughts (268)   189

Chapter Twenty-Eight:
Valuable Resource from Zdravko Lukovski (269)   191

Chapter Twenty-Nine:
Mother Teresa's Message (270)   193

Chapter Thirty:
Special Song (Using Ed Sheeran's song "Perfect")   195

Chapter Thirty-One:
"What If . . ." (276)   199

CHOOSING TRUE HAPPINESS

Chapter Thirty-Two: Grace (274)	201
Chapter Thirty-Three: Acrostic Poem for the PAST (275)	203
Chapter Thirty-Four: Acrostic Poem for the FUTURE (276)	205
Chapter Thirty-Five: Acrostic Poem for the PRESENT (277)	207
Chapter Thirty-Six: A Theme to Live By for Each Day of the Week! (278)	209
Chapter Thirty-Seven: Acrostic Poem for CHOOSE (279)	211
Chapter Thirty-Eight: The 3's (280)	213
Chapter Thirty-Nine: Morning Prayers (281)	219
Chapter Forty: Prayers at Night (282)	221
About the Author (283)	223
Endnotes (289)	227

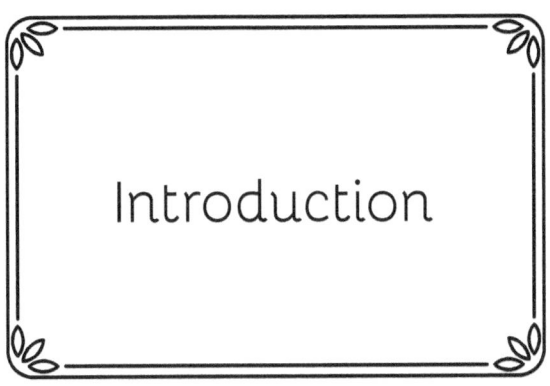

Introduction

"When I was 5 years old, my mother always told me that happiness was the key to life. When I went to school, they asked me what I wanted to be when I grew up. I wrote down 'happy.' They told me I didn't understand the assignment, and I told them they didn't understand life."
—John Lennon (1)[1]

"Happiness is the meaning and the purpose of life, the whole aim and end of human existence."
—Aristotle (2)

"If you are depressed, you are living in the past. If you are anxious, you are living in the future. If you are at peace, you are living in the present."
—Lao Tzu (3)

---

[1] The numbers in parentheses refer to the endnotes, which can be found, listed part by part and chapter by chapter, in the after-matter in the back of this book.

CHOOSING TRUE HAPPINESS

I will define happiness as "a state of mind or a feeling characterized by contentment, love, satisfaction, pleasure, or joy"[2] or "the emotional experience of having a pleasant, engaged, and meaningful life."[3]

Happiness is something that everyone wants and searches for, but not many people are able to find true happiness. True happiness is based on or influenced by someone's thoughts, feelings, words, choices, actions, and attitudes. It's up to us to know what truly makes us happy. When we know more about how our thoughts, feelings, words, choices, actions, and attitudes affect the quality of our lives, and our happiness level, we become more likely to experience meaning, satisfaction, and life-long happiness. Happiness is a choice and an achievement. It's up to you to make that happiness happen. It's not far out of reach as you may think. True happiness is definitely attainable. Perceive it! Believe it! Achieve it! If your mind can see it and believe in it, then you can do it. The powers of belief and positive thinking are extraordinary powers. You can do anything you put your mind to!

Do you want to achieve and experience true happiness? Do you want to be consistently happy throughout your life? Do you want to enjoy your life, not endure it? We all have an idea—or pretend to have one—about what happiness is. But when it comes to true happiness, we sometimes forget and pursue things like money, materialistic items, power, fame, and possessions—the things we think will lead to happiness. This will not provide you with long-term happiness. You have to know where happiness truly comes from and what will provide you with genuine, life long happiness. And choose carefully when pursuing your pleasures. Pleasure that is not connected to meaning and purpose, doesn't stay pleasurable—or promote happiness—for very long. Your pleasures should have meaning and purpose. Please keep in mind that the best things in life are free.

The ancient yoga and spiritual teachings emphasize that happiness is real only when we let go of seeking material and not lasting things and discover the long-term joy that is within. (4)

---

2 (https://en.wikipedia.org/)
3 (https://experiencelife.com/article/5-ways-to-practice-happiness/) By Joseph Hart, July 1, 2018

INTRODUCTION

All spiritual teachings are meant to make us retrace our steps to our Original Source. (Being, Awareness) We believe happiness lies elsewhere. This is a big mistake. Our essential nature is happiness.

We are all born with this natural and innate sense of happiness, that it is actually our birthright. (5)

It's important for people to be aware that their real happiness lies within themselves, that it's not dependent on something outside of them. We all need to look more deeply within ourselves. Happiness lies within and not without.

The true reality of happiness is realizing that you can achieve this intense joy any time you want, without fulfilling outer desires. You can achieve this because happiness it is in you; it's not "out there." (6)

The truth is, nothing external can buy, bring, give, or deliver happiness. You are responsible for your own happiness, and you are the only one who can create it. (7)

Happiness starts with your thinking and what you tell yourself everyday. Do you believe and identify with that voice in your head? Our minds produce a lot of mental diarrhea. Don't believe the lies. These unwanted thoughts are usually pertaining to the past or future, which only exist in our mind. Don't dwell in the past or worry about the future, concentrate your mind on the present moment. Past and future don't exist. Only the present moment exists. Choose to live your life in the present moment. Staying in the present moment takes a lot of practice. Slow, deep, focused breathing, praying, and redirecting my thoughts, attention, and mind help me to be present in the moment.

What are we here for? What is the purpose of our life? What is the aim of our life? Happiness! Happiness of course! This self-help book will give you valuable information and tools to empower yourself and strive for true happiness in your life. Hopefully, it will help you welcome each day in your life as a gift. Let happiness be the meaning and purpose of your life; make it a major priority. Tomorrow is a new day—it can also be a new beginning and a new life. My 24-hour reset button has helped me many

CHOOSING TRUE HAPPINESS

times in my life. I've learned and experienced what a difference a day can make. Time is precious and limited—spend it wisely, before it's all gone. Every day is a great opportunity for you to start anew. You are what you choose to become.

How can we achieve true happiness? In this book, I've shared my insights and experiences that have provided me with long-lasting true happiness. It's never too late to change your life around and be happy. I have learned that some days you will be happy and other days you will not be happy. That's life! My life consists of days that I enjoy and am happy. However, there are also days that I endure and struggle to get through. Some days you're the windshield and some days you're the bug. I've been the bug plenty of times. (LOL) I personally know the dark side and have experienced challenging days. Luckily, I've been happy most of the time for the past 12 years. If I was able to achieve true happiness, then you can be truly happy, too. Achieving true happiness in life is something that you deserve to experience. Happiness is your birthright! You are born to be happy!

Following the advice and information in this book each and every day will be a big step in the right direction toward your happiness journey. You'll be well on your way to achieving true happiness. Let the quest for happiness begin. Ironically, people search their entire life for happiness. And believe it or not, happiness lies within each and every one of us, we just need to access it. Once we learn and practice how to access it, happiness is always available to you. The true quality of your life is only measured by how happy and peaceful you are. The best thing you can do for this world is to be a happy, peaceful, and loving human being.

Here's my attempt to summarize my book in one sentence: To help people be happier and believe in God.

> "If you know how to handle your thoughts and emotions, there will be no such thing as anxiety, depression, stress, or tension for you."
> —Sadhguru (8)

INTRODUCTION

"We are the thinker behind the thought, the observer behind the observation, the flow of attention, the flow of awareness, the unbounded ocean of consciousness. We spontaneously realize that we have choices, and that we can exercise these choices, not through some sheer will power but spontaneously. Through meditation, we gradually bring harmony, laughter, and love back into our soul and, in the process, rediscover our unconditioned self, which can never really be lost."
—Deepak Chopra (9)

"My ultimate goal is to end up being happy. Most of the time."
—Taylor Swift (10)

CHAPTER ONE
Awareness and Being

I use these words quite often throughout the book.

Awareness

"The moment you become aware of the ego in you, it is strictly speaking no longer the ego, but just an old, conditioned mind-pattern. Ego implies unawareness. Awareness and ego cannot coexist."
—Eckhart Tolle (1)

"Awareness is the greatest agent for change."
—Eckhart Tolle (2)

* Where do you put your attention?
* Practice observing, without judgment, what's happening in the present moment.
* Give it your full attention, and just observe.
* Be thankful for it.
* The ego is identified as and attached to the mind, and conditioned by it.
* Awareness observes our False Self (Egoic Self) in action

CHOOSING TRUE HAPPINESS

Understanding the ego, identifying it within yourself, and detaching your sense of identity from it is an essential part of spiritual growth and happiness.

Reach a heightened level of awareness.

You *are* awareness. Just give up being aware of other things that are of the False Self (Egoic Self); then pure awareness alone remains, and that is the True Self.

Being

> "You are the sky. The clouds are what happens, what comes and goes."
> —Eckhart Tolle (3)

> "In today's rush, we all think too much, seek too much, want too much, and forget about the joy of just being."
> —Eckhart Tolle (4)

* Existence (like the sky)
* The nature or essence of a person
* Unconditioned Self, True Self
* That which you always are and which you always have been
* I am that I am (It is only as it is)
* Must be felt; it can't be thought
* Be, just be

Awareness and Being can be known only through experiencing them.

What is Awareness and Being?

Be aware of your True Self and experience the happiness of just being. It's all about separating the True Self (Unconditioned Self) and the False Self (Egoic Self).

I see the sky as the True Self, just there, just existing. I see the clouds, our thoughts, our emotions, as the False Self.

AWARENESS AND BEING

The beginning of all knowledge and wisdom is to know yourself. You are not your thoughts and emotions. You are the observer of your thoughts and emotions. Be aware of your thoughts, and just observe them; don't identify and react to them. Through awareness, thoughts and emotions will not become so personal. Let your thoughts and emotions pass like the clouds; allow yourself to be the sky. When you learn to be the observer, you are free. Once you know that you are not the body and not the mind, you will not suffer. You will be set free once you see the truth of who you really are!

Don't mismanage your thoughts and emotions. If you choose to do so, you will be a prisoner of your own mind. Don't allow your mind to work against you. This is what causes depression and anxiety. The whole problem with humanity is people don't know how to handle their thoughts and emotions. You must learn to manage your thoughts and emotions. And you will free yourself from being a prisoner of your own mind. You can step outside your mind anytime and be free.

Your brain likes to accept your thoughts for the truth, and your body and emotions immediately react to this "truth." This can cause you to be trapped inside of your own mind. Thoughts can run amok and become bigger and destructive. Don't be tricked—the mind is the master of all lies. Don't be ruled and controlled by your thoughts and emotions. Be in charge of your thoughts and emotions. Be free and live in the present moment, because it is a present. Because you are presence, you are a present.

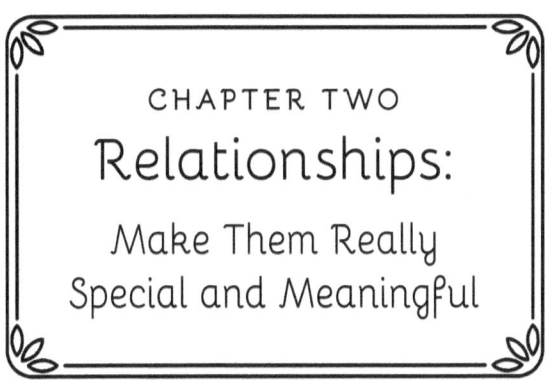

CHAPTER TWO
Relationships:
Make Them Really Special and Meaningful

"Time decides who you meet in life, your heart decides who you want in your life, and your behavior decides who stays in your life."
—Ziad K. Abdelnour (1)

I will define relationships as, "connections, associations, or involvements between people."[4]

From the moment we're born to the moment we die, relationships exist in our life. Relationships are crucial to the level of happiness that we'll achieve during our lifetime. The more positive relationships we have in our life, the more happiness we can experience. The more negative relationships we have in our life, the less happiness we can experience. Relationships shape us. They help define us. They help create a part of who we are. They affect our thinking, emotions, words, and actions. They affect our whole being, especially our well-being.

---

[4] www.dictionary.com

CHOOSING TRUE HAPPINESS

Relationships give meaning and purpose to our lives. Relationships connect us to people and things. They can give us the opportunity to love and be loved. Love is the most powerful emotion and is key to happiness. So, if relationships are so important to our happiness, why not create positive, special, meaningful, and healthy relationships? Focus on relationships that we want to create and maintain.

Yes, effort is involved to a certain extent. Successful relationships require a lot of giving, not taking. However, the benefits that are reaped are well worth the effort. Care and attention to the key relationships in your life will pay off tremendously. Make a great choice and spend some time every day to connect with God and the important people in your life. I make sure that I spend some quality time with God and my daughters every day. Look for good opportunities to interact with others in a positive, engaging, and meaningful way. Even if it's only for a few minutes. I developed a nice relationship with the crossing guard, Sophia, at my school. The relationship started by saying "Good morning" to one another. After that, some days we would chat for a few minutes in the morning. Throughout your lifetime, you will have numerous opportunities to have positive, engaging, and meaningful interactions with people.

How you feel about life often comes down to how you feel about your relationships. We are created to have relationships. In order to have a good life, our relationships need to be balanced and healthy. But, way too often, we ignore the most important relationship—our spiritual connection with God.

Relationships are vital for our overall well-being and happiness level. The better the quality of our relationships, the better the quality of our life. The quality of your relationships has an enormous effect on the quality of your life. We all have a great need for companionship. Acknowledge this, and do not go through your life trying to find other things to replace companionship. Sometimes the greatest relationships are the ones you never expected to be in.

In order to be in a positive, healthy relationship, you need to be comfortable with who you are. You need to love and respect yourself before you can truly love and respect anybody else.

RELATIONSHIPS: MAKE THEM REALLY SPECIAL...

Relationships don't just happen—we create them. Value and appreciate the good relationships you have in your life. A positive, connected relationship with your family or another human being may bring you much happiness. Do a lot of networking. Meet a lot of people. The more people you meet, the better chance you have of meeting quality people and establishing quality relationships. Quality relationships can open many wonderful doors for you:

* Spiritual Growth—God First and Foremost
* Partnerships (Think often about how lucky you are to have found your partner. This is something I need to do more often.)
* Children
* Friendships
* Careers
* Pets (Especially dogs)
* Fun
* Financial Growth
* HAPPINESS

All quality relationships require some time and effort. Regardless of whatever relationship you're in, show that you care and express interest on a daily basis. It takes only a minute to leave a note on a table or in a room for a special someone. Every relationship should have a unique bond that makes the relationship special.

I believe the key ingredients in quality relationships are love, trust, respect, communication, understanding, patience, honesty, commitment, teamwork, empathy, dependability, compromising, attention, and forgiveness—all two-way streets. I can definitely benefit from better communication and more patience and understanding in my marriage. Sometimes I feel my wife and I are speaking two different languages to one another. (lol!) One thing I learned in my marriage is to enjoy the ups and get through the downs. Relationships can definitely have ups and downs. Make the relationships that you have in your life work for you, not against you. This will bring you joy, rather than pain. Say kind words to one another. If you have difficulty verbalizing kind words, then write them down. Compliments, praise, and appreciation work very well. You will get a lot of mileage out of saying positive things every day.

Think before you speak. If you don't have anything nice to say, then don't say anything at all. Show reassurance to your partner; hopefully, it will be reciprocated. Support one another, and, when needed, lift each other up. Make your partner feel respected and loved. Create special moments and memories. Reflect on those moments and memories. Reminisce! Relationships are a huge part of our lives. Relationships are key to our happiness. So, create loving, strong, solid relationships throughout your lifetime.

You can use your faith, career, pets, hobbies, sports, libraries, educational institutions, fitness centers, the arts, and social media to create positive relationships. Most importantly, be fulfilled spiritually through your religion, your prayers, and your relationship with God. Relationships bring special meaning to our lives. They can guide us in the present and the future. Relationships can enhance the present, amend the past, and touch the future. They can give us love, hope, help, strength, direction, courage, determination, and persistence. Relationships can help to plan and build our future. They can provide us with the all-important sense of *belonging*. They can help us establish an identity.

Reflect on and think about the relationships you have in your life. What can you do to improve the relationship? What can the other person do to improve the relationship? Make plans to improve the relationship now—right now! What can you do to allow the relationship to flourish? What can the other person do to allow the relationship to flourish? Make arrangements to do it now. Right now! Showing appreciation is a great place to start allowing relationships to improve and flourish. Appreciation builds strong relationships.

Don't be afraid to leave a negative relationship. Be courageous, *and just do it*. When one door closes, another one opens. The new door will never open unless you close the old door. Nothing will change until you close the door. Slam it shut, and don't look back! Make any necessary changes in order to allow the new door to open. Life is too short; keep poisonous, negative people and toxic relationships out of your life. And don't fall into the trap of thinking you

RELATIONSHIPS: MAKE THEM REALLY SPECIAL ...

must have somebody in order to be happy. There are plenty of single, happy people out there. Regardless of anybody's opinion, there is absolutely nothing wrong with being single. It's much better to be single rather than being miserable in a relationship. Being single were some of the happiest times of my life.

Get up now, and go do something that will foster positive relationships. Make it a daily routine to think and reflect about the relationships in your life and how you can create the best, most satisfying relationships. Choose your relationships wisely.

I try my best to treat all the people I come across with the utmost respect and kindness. Respect and kindness are languages that the blind can see and the deaf can hear. Now, *that's* powerful. Treating people with respect and kindness can allow you to build positive, healthy relationships. And everybody likes to be treated with respect and kindness. Think of the Golden Rule: Treat people the way you want to be treated.

The most important relationship in my life is the relationship I have with God. That's my priority, and it should be everyone's number-one priority. Ultimately, we are all God's children. Each day, I strive to love God with all my mind, heart, and soul, and to love my neighbor as myself. Every day, I want to be the best person that I can possibly be and bring honor and glory to God in how I think and feel and in what I say and do. Some days I'm successful, other days I'm not. (lol!) Your relationship with God is the most important relationship you will ever have here on this Earth. It should be number one on your list and your matter of greatest importance.

The second most important relationship in your life is with yourself. You will live with yourself for your entire life. Everyone has their own internal struggles. The biggest battle of all is the one within yourself. And it all starts with your thinking. Make your mind work for you, not against you. You can choose to be your own best friend or own worst enemy. The choice is yours and yours alone. Don't put yourself down or beat yourself up. Learn to respect and love yourself. How do you feel about yourself? Do you respect and love yourself?

Other positive, healthy and fulfilling relationships in my life involve being a father, husband, son, grandson, nephew, great nephew, cousin, son-in-law,

CHOOSING TRUE HAPPINESS

brother-in-law, dog dad, friend, school counselor, and neighbor. My *nonno* and *nonna* taught me, with their words and actions, to be nice to everyone and that, if I do that, everything will fall into place. Quality relationships will pass the ultimate test of time. I make it a strong point not to have any negative relationships in my life, and I never stay on bad terms with anybody. I'm very blessed to have many fulfilling and loving relationships in my life. These types of relationships contribute to me being truly happy.

Are you ready to make the necessary choices and put forth effort to create positive, loving, healthy, and fulfilling relationships? What choices and efforts will you put forth to create positive, loving, healthy, and fulfilling relationships? What would life be without relationships? Relationships aren't about how much love there is in the beginning. Rather, they are about how much love there is in the end.

> "I'm not telling you it is going to be easy.
> I am telling you it is going to be worth it."
> —Art L. Williams, Jr. (2)

> "Don't let negative and toxic people rent space in your head. Raise the rent and kick them out."
> —Zig Ziglar (3)

> "I want you to be concerned about your next-door neighbor. Do you know your next-door neighbor?"
> —Mother Teresa (4)

CHAPTER THREE

Appreciation:

Think It, Feel It, and Show It Often

"Gratitude unlocks the fullness of life. It turns what we have into enough—and more. It turns denial into acceptance, chaos to order, confusion to clarity. It can turn a meal into a feast, a house into a home, a stranger into a friend."
—MELODY BEATTIE (1)

I will define appreciation as "recognition of the quality, value, significance, or magnitude of people and things."[5]

A heartfelt thank you to all the brave men and women who have served or are serving our country. And a very special thanks to their families. Our military and their families have made tremendous sacrifices. Many who served have made the ultimate sacrifice. Our military and their families are and always will be our Greatest Heroes. Our military personnel have made it possible for all of us to enjoy our freedom and maintain our lifestyle. Let's always remember that on a daily basis by keeping our greatest heroes in our

---

5 www.yourdictionary.com

prayers, hearts, and minds. Show them appreciation, love, kindness, and generosity. I wish I could list the name of every single person who has served our country (approximately 40 million people have served). Please don't take your freedom for granted—it's not free.

Ahhh, it's so nice to say "Thank you" and be appreciative. It's beneficial to express and show what we're grateful for in our lives. If you and your loved ones are lucky enough to be healthy, then be grateful. Your health is your greatest wealth. Verbalize appreciation! Words of praise are free and worth their weight in gold. Show appreciation! Use compliments and enthusiasm. Think of appreciation often. Show appreciation often! It will make you—and others—feel good.

Keep a gratitude journal. Write a gratitude letter to someone. Make a list of all the things that you're grateful and thankful for in your life. The list might surprise you. Read the list every day. Try as much as possible not to take things for granted. Thank you very much (lol!).

Appreciate even your challenges or obstacles because they are guiding you on the path of life and helping to build your character. In the middle of difficulty lies opportunity. Every twist, turn, and miraculous detour has its purpose. Even when there's pain, know that it's for the best, because you will grow as you are put to the test. Pain = Growth. Struggle brings strength.

Too many people tend to focus their mind on what they *don't* have rather than being grateful for what they *do* have. This will not bring happiness if you choose to do this, it will bring you unhappiness. Gratitude will shift your focus from what you do not have to what you do have. Focus your mind on what you do have, and increase your happiness level. Count your blessings, rather than your burdens. Have and maintain a thankful mindset. This will help you to be a happier person.

Unfortunately, people take too many things for granted. And sometimes you don't realize what you have until it's gone. Therefore, be appreciative while you still have it. Furthermore, a lot of humans have a tendency to complain a lot. Don't complain about people, things, or situations. Many people on this Earth didn't even live long enough to complain. Complaining is a total waste of time and energy. Replace complaining with appreciation. Be grateful for what you have in your life. Thank you very much. (lol!)

APPRECIATION: THINK IT, FEEL IT, AND SHOW IT OFTEN

Appreciate all the people who have touched your life. Let them know about it. Appreciate all the educators you've had in your life. Find them, and let them know how they touched your life. Develop a whole different level of appreciation for all the people and things in your life. Thank you very much. (lol!)

Think of a time in your life when you were down and out—lost in life. Then, that special someone was there to give you the lift that you so desperately needed. Be extremely grateful. Certain people come into your life at a certain time and for a certain reason. We need to be aware of this and definitely appreciate it. Michael M. Gemellaro was one of those people for me. At the time, he knew I was struggling. So, he grabbed me by both shoulders, gently shook them, looked me in the eye, and said, "What are you doing?" It was a wake-up call and spark that I really needed. Thank you, Slim.

Those of us who have a thankful mind and heart have taken a big step forward for living a happy life. There are so many things in your life and in this world to be thankful for. Create and maintain an attitude of gratitude for yourself.

Appreciate all the things you have in your life. Regardless of what you have, appreciate it. The greatest of riches is to be content with little. Less is more. True happiness will not be attained by wanting more and more—it might even cause unhappiness. However, true happiness can be attained by being content with what you have and realizing what you have. If you can live contently with little, then you are truly wealthy. Sometimes, you don't realize what you have until it is gone. Realize what you have before it's gone. Appreciation, gratitude, and thankfulness don't always come naturally—we need to practice these things. The science behind appreciation, gratitude, and thankfulness shows many benefits for our physical and mental well-being, including socially and emotionally.

Unfortunately, taking things for granted is a part of human nature. It's important to realize what we have in our lives while we still have it. Focus on what you have, not on what you don't have. Count all your blessings daily. Thank God for this moment and this day that you have.

CHOOSING TRUE HAPPINESS

Say *Thank you* on a daily basis. Be thankful on a daily basis; don't wait for a holiday. Make a list of everything that you are thankful for. Use appreciation as a super-power and super-tool that you possess and can use at will, whenever you want. It's free and very powerful. An unappreciative life is an empty and sad life.

When you get out of bed in the morning and your feet hit the floor, be appreciative and grateful. There are a lot of people who don't have that opportunity. Most days when I get out of bed, I watch my feet hit the floor, and I think to myself, *Thank you, God, for another day.* Then I walk over to a large pair of wooden rosary beads, make the Sign of the Cross, and kiss the cross that has Jesus's face on it. It's a great way to start the day.

People yearn for appreciation. People want to be recognized and acknowledged. The best way to receive appreciation is to give it. Appreciation can make somebody's day; it can even change someone's life. All you have to do is express it. I do understand that it's not always easy to do, however, try your best.

We are all so busy, constantly on the go. We are often so caught up in our destination that we forget to appreciate the journey—the little things, the big things, and all the other things in between on our journey. Stop and take a slow, deep, focused breath. Take some time to smell the fresh air and enjoy nature. Enjoy the journey, and let the destination be worth it. Let the journey and the destination have purpose. Make sure the prize is worth the fight. What is the purpose of your journey and destination?

Miracles are everywhere. Miracles happen every day. I see miracles everywhere. Do you believe in miracles? I hope so, because *you are a miracle*. I am a miracle. Appreciate life itself. Appreciate the miracle of life. Live your life as though everything is a miracle! Believe in miracles!

Often, life is lived forward and understood backwards. Living life forward and understanding it backwards can help you reflect, learn, and grow. Hindsight is 20/20. Mistakes are okay to make as long as you learn from your mistakes. Make great choices, and understand and appreciate life as much as possible while you are living it in the present moment.

APPRECIATION: THINK IT, FEEL IT, AND SHOW IT OFTEN

Next time you turn on the electricity or water and take a shower, be very grateful. Many millions of people don't have the luxuries of electricity and/or running water. Next time you sit down to eat, be very grateful. Hundreds of millions of people don't have enough food. Next time you walk through the door of your home, be grateful. Many millions of people don't have a place they can call home.

When you appreciate the people in your life, you increase your happiness level and their happiness level. When you appreciate things in your life, you make those things special, more meaningful, and more valuable.

Appreciation is a key component to any effective relationship. One of the best ways to improve a relationship is to show appreciation. A great tool to make yourself and others feel good is appreciation. Pick a person, and make a list of all the things that you appreciate in that person.

Appreciation allows us to live a complete and full life. It allows us to be content with what we have. It can magnify what we have in our life. It allows us to live life with acceptance.

Appreciation is a choice. It should be practiced until it comes naturally to you. I'm still waiting for it to come naturally to me. (lol!) The more you show it, the better you get at it. Being appreciative will make you and others feel better.

Gratitude is beneficial and powerful. It is consistently and strongly associated with greater happiness. Gratitude helps people be more optimistic and feel more positive emotions. It can make us healthier, happier, kinder, and friendlier. Gratitude actually feels good. How appreciative you are is directly related to greater happiness.

Create a gratitude list, and document it in some way, such as using a notebook. Whatever you choose, make sure that it is something you will use and refer to regularly, so make it easy to access.

Think of one thing to be grateful for each day, and add to the list daily. Stick with it every day, and keep thinking of something you are grateful for. Once you think of one thing, it becomes easier to think of other things to add to the list. At the end of a week, you will already have seven things that you are grateful for.

CHOOSING TRUE HAPPINESS

A good prompt is: "Today, I am grateful for . . ."

Examples: I am healthy. I can see. I have a home. My talents are . . . I have a family. I love music. I have food and water, and I have internet access.

Always use bullet points or some other form of listing that works for you, and keep the items short and to the point.

Keep the gratitude list up to date. The things for which you are grateful will change over time, and that is as it should be, for *you* change as well. Look at the list, and read it often. Start creating a gratitude list today—you'll be happy that you chose to do so! Show and maintain an attitude of gratitude.

The time to be appreciative of everything in your life is now. Time is a precious commodity. Unfortunately, many people don't realize and appreciate how valuable time is until it's gone. Take the time to be grateful in this present moment. Gratitude is so powerful that it can shift your perceptions, thoughts, and feelings, and make you see your world in a different way. Once you practice and become really good at expressing gratitude, it will make you focus on the positive. An amazing gift of appreciation is that *the more appreciative you are, the more present you become.* And living in the present moment is everything.

I'm thankful for being a part of:

1. God's Family
2. My Family
3. The SEEALL Academy, PS/IS 180 Family/District 20 Family
4. St. Clare Parish (Staten Island) Family
5. St. Joseph Hill Academy High School (Staten Island) Family
6. Great Kills Swim Club Family (GKSC)
7. 1106 Design Family
8. K-LOVE 95.5 FM (I love Skip, Amy, Carlos, and Lauree!!!)
9. Xaverian High School Family

What families are you thankful for being a part of?

APPRECIATION: THINK IT, FEEL IT, AND SHOW IT OFTEN

Do you have an appreciative attitude? Do you have a thankful mind and heart? Have you expressed appreciation for everything that you have in your life? What are you waiting for? Now is the time!

Here is my gratitude list (it's always a work-in-progress). I'm thankful for my:

* Spiritual Growth and God
* Health
* Freedom (special thanks to our military and their families)
* Wife (Super Wife, Super Mom, Super Cook, Super Assistant Principal)
* Two beautiful daughters, Isabella and Olivia
* Wonderful Mom
* Dad, especially the many hard lessons I learned from his life
* Grandparents (especially *Nonno* and *Nonna*)
* Aunts (especially Angela and Diane)
* Uncles (especially Joel and Steve—great role models)
* Cousins (especially Frankie, Steven, Catherine, Michael, Theo, Ben [also my godson], and Maggie)
* Nephew (Joseph)
* Niece (Nicolette)
* Father-in-law (Dino), mother-in-law (Roseann), brother-in-law (Joe), and sister-in-law (Bernadette)—the best in-laws ever
* Pet dog, Teddy
* Friends, including the Regina Pacis Crew and Maple Lanes Boyz, I love you guys!
* Friends, John and Jen, and their children Julianna and Nicholas
* Friends, Alex and Roseann, and their children Alex and my goddaughter Cristina
* Home
* Luxuries in my house (lights, running water, heat, AC, hot shower, refrigerator with a lot of food, dishwasher, washer, and dryer
* Job (students, colleagues, and administration)
* Connection to all of nature

CHOOSING TRUE HAPPINESS

* Loving heart
* Ability to take a slow, deep, focused breath
* God-given ability to write this book

Who are the people that you appreciate in your life? How have you expressed that appreciation to them? What are the things that you have in your life that you appreciate? Do you think of those things often?

> "Gratitude, like faith, is a muscle. The more you use it, the stronger it grows, and the more power you have to use it on your behalf. If you do not practice gratefulness, its benefaction will go unnoticed, and your capacity to draw on its gifts will be diminished. To be grateful is to find blessings in everything. This is the most powerful attitude to adopt, for there are blessings in everything."
> —ALAN COHEN (2)

> "There are only two ways to live your life. One is as though nothing is a miracle. The other is as though everything is a miracle."
> —ALBERT EINSTEIN (3)

> "Showing gratitude is one of the simplest, yet most powerful, things humans can do for each other."
> —RANDY RAUSCH (4)

CHAPTER FOUR
Perspective:
Keep It Positive, Please

"With everything that has happened to you, you can either feel sorry for yourself or treat what has happened as a gift. Everything is either an opportunity to grow or an obstacle to keep you from growing. You get to choose."
—Dr. Wayne Dyer (1)

Your perception of your life, life events, and life itself is crucial in achieving true happiness. You can choose to change the way you see things. This is an extremely powerful tool you can use throughout your lifetime. Things may be much better than you might think. If you change the way you think about or view something, then that something already is better. A change in perception can lead to amazing results in your life.

There are many different ways to look at all the events that take place in life. Be open-minded and positive as much as possible. Ask yourself, "How can I use this as something positive?" You always have the choice to turn a negative into a positive. For example, after dealing with depression and anxiety at different times in my life, I chose to write this book. Another example is working on this book during a pandemic. You can find the positive in just about everything.

If you change the way you see things, then the things you see change. For example, pretend you wake up one morning, and it is pouring rain outside. Some responses might be: *Wow, it is pouring outside. I'm going to get soaked today. I don't even know where the umbrella is. I don't even know if I have an umbrella. What a way to start the day.* All these responses don't look at the rain in a positive way. Now let's say you change your perception on how you view the rain. Let's pretend you choose one of these responses: *Thank God it's raining; the grass, trees, plants, and flowers need the water to survive. Thank God it's raining—our reservoirs are filling up. Thank God it rains around here; there are some areas of the world that are very dry and don't receive the rain they need. Look at how beautiful those raindrops look. Listen to the beautiful sound the raindrops make when they land. How about laughing at getting wet in the rain? Thank God for this rain, because, without it, life wouldn't be possible.*

Do you see how you can change the way you see the rain? Next time it is pouring rain outside, try to choose one of the positive responses, and think of the rain in a positive way. Once you do that, you change the way you see the rain, therefore, the rain you see has changed. You have the power to use a positive perspective in all parts of your life. You can change the way you see everything. You can choose your frame of mind in every situation. See every situation as it is. Try as much as possible not to add your opinions and judgments. I know firsthand that this is definitely not easy to do.

You can change the way you see yourself. Don't be so hard on yourself; think about your positive traits and accomplishments. Furthermore, instead of complaining about petty things, which is what we humans so often do, stop complaining. Let's count our blessings, daily and consistently. Use the gratitude list previously mentioned. Try not to do what our minds love to do, which is complain, criticize, and compare (The 3 Cs). Challenge yourself to try to make it through one full day without verbalizing one of The 3 Cs. You might get a good laugh taking this challenge. I haven't made it through too many days not using 1 of the 3 Cs. (lol!)

PERSPECTIVE: KEEP IT POSITIVE, PLEASE

You can change the way you see others. For example, instead of talking about and noticing people's negative qualities, focus on their positive qualities instead. It's certainly easier to look at a person's negative qualities. However, reflect and take a step back and notice that person's positive qualities. If you are reflecting now about a particular person and thinking to yourself, *That person doesn't have any positive qualities*, then you are probably doing it again—looking at that person's negative qualities.

I know some people often choose to exhibit their negative qualities quite often. This is when you really need to make a strong effort and try extra hard to focus on that person's positive qualities. I can tell you from personal experience that this is very challenging to do. At times, I've been successful doing this, however, many times I've been unsuccessful. I think it is human nature to notice negative qualities in a person. This starts at a young age. People complimenting others is not seen or heard of as often as people judging, complaining about, criticizing, comparing, and insulting others.

Make a resolution to yourself to start focusing on other people's positive qualities. I know it can be a difficult task, but resolve to look at the positive qualities of that person instead of the negative qualities. Remember: You can choose how you perceive that person. If you change the way you see a person, then that person changes (of course, in your mind and eyes).

You can change the way you see situations. For example, let's say you are stuck in traffic. Some responses might be: *This !*!!* traffic! I'm so sick of it! When are they going to fix it already? I'm going to be late again! This construction never ends! What are they working on now? I don't even see anybody working.*

Now let's say you changed your perception of being stuck in traffic. Let's pretend you choose one of these responses: *Thank God I'm stuck in this traffic. Lots of people would love the opportunity to be stuck in this traffic. Thank God I'm stuck in this traffic and not serving in a war overseas. I'm not going to stress over things that I can't control. Thank God I'm in this traffic and not in a hospital fighting a serious illness, like many others my age are doing. I can't control the traffic; when I get there, I get there.*

CHOOSING TRUE HAPPINESS

Yes, you can't control the traffic, however, you can control how you respond and view the situation of being stuck in traffic. If you change the way you see the traffic, then the traffic you see changes. You will see the traffic in a whole different light, and it might not be so bad after all. Do not stress over things you can't control.

One morning, there was a major accident on the Verrazzano Bridge. My usual commute to work is about an hour. However, this particular morning, it took me about 3.5 hours. So how did I react to this situation? How did I deal with this traffic? I chose to remain calm and have a positive perspective. I really surprised myself that I was able to stay calm and positive.

I did a lot of slow, deep, focused breathing, reminded myself that a lot of people would love to be in this traffic, looked around at nature, and sang and listened to music. When I arrived at work, I was very relaxed and smiling and had a great day.

My wife, on the other hand, was getting frustrated and kept calling me from her SUV. She was saying things like, "How much longer is it going to be?" "I'm turning back—I can't take this anymore." "Can I make a U-turn and go a different way, a quicker way?" At the moment, she wasn't in a good frame of mind. She lost her patience and was getting stressed and frustrated, which I have also done many times.

Another technique you can use is ask yourself, "Will this matter in an hour, a day, or a week?" The answer is *No, it will not matter*. It's healthier and safer to laugh than to get angry and possibly put yourself or others in a harmful and dangerous situation. Currently the method I use with irresponsible drivers is that I think to myself, *One team, many destinations*. This means that I view all the drivers on the road as part of my team. And we all have our own destinations.

However, it takes teamwork for everyone to arrive safe and sound. So, if someone cuts me off, I have to view them as part of my team, and they need my help to get to their destination. So, it's okay if they cut me off because they are on my team, and we all need to arrive safely at our destinations. And why take it personally when you don't even know if it was deliberate? The easy thing

PERSPECTIVE: KEEP IT POSITIVE, PLEASE

to do is take it personally and get frustrated and angry. Do the harder thing and think or say, *One team, many destinations.* How you view the situation is more important than the situation itself.

Please note that these techniques to tame road rage were discovered after making mistakes and losing my cool behind the wheel. I experienced a couple of incidences of road rage which involved a very heated verbal exchange that could have turned out really bad. Please learn from my mistakes, and use a technique that works for you and helps you to keep your cool behind the wheel.

How you perceive what happens to you in your life is extremely important for living a happy and healthy life. How we perceive what happens to us in our lives is actually more important than the event itself. I can't emphasize this enough. If you change the way you look at things, then those things change in your eyes and mind. You can find the positive in almost any situation. Make your experiences life lessons—live and learn. Some positives can even arise—eventually—out of the worst tragedies in the world. Choose to make the best of the current situation.

Nobody on this Earth will be happy all the time. And life is not about being happy all the time. However, we should try our best to be happy most of the time. We, as human beings, have a wide array of emotions for many reasons—one may be to make changes or to learn from a mistake.

Don't ignore, avoid, or repress any pain in your life. If you do, you may turn to gambling, alcohol, drugs, or other harmful activities. These vices may temporarily numb you and provide an escape for the time being. However, deep down inside, the pain will still be there and might even become worse. Therefore, confront your pain head on, and deal with it directly. You have the strength and courage to make a good choice and work through your pain. Determination and persistence will conquer most things.

You are allowed to feel whatever it is that you are feeling. Feelings are not *right* or *wrong*—they are just feelings. Fight your negativity with all your being. Choose not to listen to the negative voice in your head, which I call "brain farts." Choose to laugh at and ignore the negative voice in your head.

CHOOSING TRUE HAPPINESS

Then find one positive thing about the person or situation that is upsetting you. When the mind is afflicting us, this can be a great opportunity to practice appreciation, gratitude, and thankfulness. Don't let your mind continue to cause you pain and suffering. Don't identify and react to the mind when it produces negative thoughts. Your time is precious and limited. You don't want to waste it being controlled by that negative voice in your head.

If you change the way you see things, you can create your own, positive, perspective. You can put a positive spin on almost anything. The day that you feel off is when you really need to realize that life is a precious blessing. Do you remember your thoughts and perspective the last time it poured rain, you were stuck in traffic, or someone cut you off? Did you remain calm and maintain a positive perspective, or did you get upset, angry, or frustrated? Start training your mind to see people, things, and situations from a positive perspective. Positivity is a choice. Now, after making many mistakes, I try my best to see everything from a positive perspective.

Life is all about how we look at it. This is how I choose to look at life.

* Precious gift from God
* Miracle
* Struggle
* Celebration
* Journey that's challenging and beautiful
* Difficult and unpredictable (nobody said it would be easy) (lol!)
* Full of possibilities
* Learning experience
* Fun adventure
* Roller-coaster ride, with ups and downs
* Opportunity to fulfill my purpose and destiny

PERSPECTIVE: KEEP IT POSITIVE, PLEASE

Look at this word:
IMPOSSIBLE.
What do you see?
"IMPOSSIBLE"
or
"I'M POSSIBLE"?
I see I'M POSSIBLE, and I hope you do, too.

What about this phrase?
HAPPINESSISNOWHERE.
What do you see?
HAPPINESS IS NO WHERE
or
"HAPPINESS IS NOW HERE"?
I see HAPPINESS IS NOW HERE, and I hope you do, too.

"Gratitude turns what we have into enough."
—Anonymous (2)

"Much in life is simply a matter of perspective. It's not inherently good or bad, a success or failure; it's how we choose to look at things that makes the difference."
—David Niven (3)

"The way I define happiness is being the creator of your experience, choosing to take pleasure in what you have, right now, regardless of the circumstances, while being the best you that you can be."
—Leo Babauta (4)

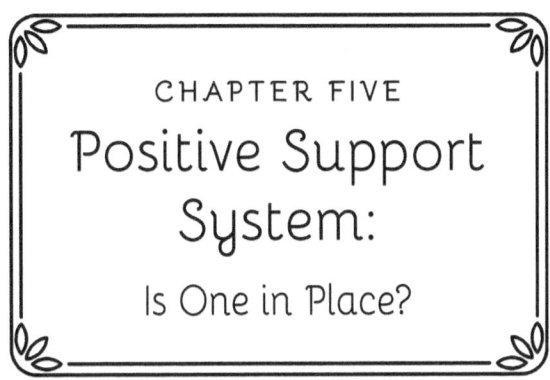

CHAPTER FIVE
Positive Support System:
Is One in Place?

"The goal is to build up the wall of positivity so high around you that, no matter what negativity comes your way, it can't get through but bounces off and no longer affects your well-being."
—Sharon R. Hutchinson (1)

Sooner or later, at some point in your life, you will need to turn to and utilize the assistance of a positive support system. A positive support system can really help you get through the challenging and difficult times. It can help you to see the brighter days that lie ahead. We must remember that all negative emotion is temporary. This too shall pass. There is light at the end of the tunnel. A positive support system will help you see that light. Reaching out for help for yourself or others is a sign of honesty, intelligence, strength, and courage.

Your positive support system may include, but is not limited to: Your faith, praying, exercise, deep breathing (slow and focused), family, friends, neighbors, proper nutrition, favorite physical activities, therapists, doctors, nutritionists, meditation, herbs, vitamins, natural supplements, reading, nature,

CHOOSING TRUE HAPPINESS

medications, colleagues, pets (especially a dog), music, hobbies, special talents, singing, dancing, drawing, massage, art, yoga classes, herbal teas, wines, books, a warm tub, or a nap. At the end of this section, I've shared a list of things I use or have used for a successful positive support system.

I strongly feel that one of the best things you can do for yourself during your lifetime is to get a dog. Adopt, don't shop. October is National Adopt a Shelter Dog Month. Your life will change for the better in ways you have never, ever imagined. It's definitely no coincidence that God spelled backwards is "dog." My Mini Golden Doodle Teddy is like a son to me—I love him so, so, so much. The only living creature that will love you more than you love yourself is a dog.

Surround yourself with positive people. Surround yourself with positive energy. Your positive side will increase and feed off that energy and those people. Be sure to make your inner circle very special. Make sure you know your inner circle very well. Surround yourself with winners. Stay away from negative people and negative energy. Misery loves company. Make company with winners who are positive and energetic.

A positive support system can give us hope, help, faith, strength, courage, knowledge, direction, and peace of mind. It can improve our happiness level. It can provide us with a safety cushion that can be comforting and relieving. It's important to have a positive support system in place for life's storms.

Many people hit rock bottom at a certain point in their life. It's not about how many times you fall down—it's about how many times you get back up. I have fallen plenty of times and always got back up, regardless of how long it took. Sometimes, it was quick, and, other times, it took much longer. However, I never threw in the towel and gave up. Remember: Nothing ever stays the same.

Think to yourself—often, *This will work out* or *Everything works out*, and never, ever lose hope. There's always hope, help, and faith. Everyone has a story. How you interpret and respond to it means everything. Let go of your story and all the unnecessary drama around it—just drop it. It's just a story you keep repeating, like a broken record. It's not the essence of who you are. You are *being* and *awareness*.

POSITIVE SUPPORT SYSTEM: IS ONE IN PLACE?

It's okay to reach out for help. We all have something that we can improve. Getting help for yourself and/or others is a sign of honesty, intelligence, strength, and courage. Everybody needs help at one point or another in their life. And that's all good. As Michael Phelps said, "It's okay to not be okay."

Having a positive support system in place will allow a person to bounce back a lot faster. Once you know what is causing your unhappiness, then it's time to create a positive support system and take effective and immediate action to make some changes.

Change is good. When the system is in place, and you know what works for you, you can use it for the rest of your life. Take the time and make the effort to build the right positive support system that works for you. You will always have it to fall back on, which can be very reassuring. Therefore, it's definitely worth the time and effort to establish a positive support system. A positive support system will provide the opportunity for you to live a happier and more fulfilling life. Do you have a positive support system in place that works well for you? What does your positive support system look like? Be accountable to yourself for creating, following, and maintaining a positive support system.

What are some things I use or have used for my positive support system?

* God, praying, my faith
* Exercising
* Meditation using slow, deep, focused breathing (I love using the Smiling Mind App!)
* Family
* Lots of laughing
* My pet dog, Teddy
* Friends
* Therapists (Thank you Alyse and Marie, I love you!)
* My diet
* Doctors
* Medication

CHOOSING TRUE HAPPINESS

- Vitamins
- Natural supplements
- Reading
- Admiring nature
- Job (students, colleagues, and administration)
- Music that especially connects me to God (I listen to 95.5 Positive Encouraging K-LOVE. I love that radio station!)
- Chess
- Singing and Dancing
- Professional massages
- Chamomile and Matcha Green Tea
- Red wine
- Books
- Walnuts, dark chocolate (minimum 70%), lemon water, avocados, blueberries, and kiwis
- Internet for research (For spiritual growth and overall well-being)

"Happiness is not something you postpone for the future; it is something you design for the present."
—JIM ROHN (2)

"Positive thoughts, positive actions, positive results!"
—LISA BOEHNING (3)

"When you have a strong support system, you have the freedom to express yourself in whatever capacity you can."
—SHWETA MENON (4)

CHAPTER SIX
I Agree—It's Up to Me.
I Am My Own Biggest Project.

> "Everything you have in your life, you have attracted to yourself because of the way you think, because of the person that you are. You can change your life because you can change the way you think."
> —BRIAN TRACY (1)

The I is for you. It all starts with you. You create your own happiness. You make your own happiness. Obviously, none of this could happen without you being comfortable with who you are. Wouldn't it be great if you could tell yourself frequently, *I love who I am.* Wouldn't it be wonderful to recite such positive affirmations on a daily basis? Remember, your brain believes what you tell it. For example, after taking a slow, deep, focused breath, try saying softly, out loud, "I am relaxed" or "I am calm." I hope you reap the same amazing benefits that I do.

You can be your own best friend or your own worst enemy. You decide! Our lives are shaped by the choices that we make. Granted, some people get dealt harder hands, but our lives are still defined by the choices that we make.

CHOOSING TRUE HAPPINESS

Make it a point to build yourself up, not tear yourself down! When I was going through my anxiety, I was tearing myself down. This choice caused me to suffer on and off for a few years.

Make sure what you think, feel, say, and do are all in harmony with one another. Your thinking, feelings, and actions are all connected and related to one another. Your thinking affects your feelings and actions. Your feelings affect your thinking and actions. And your actions affect your thinking and feelings. Each one affects the other two, however, it all starts with your thinking. Think with your heart and free mind (see chart in this section). Make sure your heart and free mind are in sync with one another. Use the power of positive thinking. Positive thinking is extremely powerful. Put it to work for you. Your actions and emotions that follow the positive thinking should be pleasing.

Use the law of attraction to attract positive things into your life. Use mental imagery to visualize what you want. Close your eyes and picture it. After you visualize what you want, go out there and get it.

You are going to need to stay focused and put forth the appropriate and necessary effort in order to be successful. Therefore, in the long run, your results will be directly connected to your effort level. Do the best job you can with the task at hand. Say to yourself, "I'm going to do it as well as possible." Let your life's purpose lead to your goals and your goals lead to your priorities. Find something that lights your fire and about which you are passionate. The potential for *greatness* lives within each of us. Find that *greatness* in *you*. *Nothing* can shut the light out that shines from inside you.

Know yourself, be yourself, believe in yourself, and love yourself. It's important to know yourself—especially your strengths and weaknesses. Build on your strengths, and improve your weaknesses. Be honest and true to yourself. Live true to yourself. Do the right thing. Don't live a life of lies. This will not get you anywhere you really want to be. Remember, when you tell the truth, you don't need to remember everything you said. Be yourself; live the life that *you* want to lead, not the life that others want you to lead. Live the life you love, and love the life you live. Believe in yourself. You are capable of achieving whatever you want to achieve. If you believe in yourself,

I AGREE—IT'S UP TO ME . . .

show determination and persistence, and work hard, then anything is possible. When people tell you that you can't, show them that you can. Silence the doubters and critics!!! Most importantly, love yourself. You are God's gift and creation—you are a miracle.

Keep in mind that, ultimately, we are all responsible for our own lives. If you choose to say kind words and give compliments and encouragement, then start with others. If you choose to judge, criticize and point the finger, then start in the mirror. Remember that your choices have consequences. What you choose to say and do will affect not only *your* life but the lives of other people. Therefore, be careful in what you say and do. Think before you speak or act. Choose your words and actions toward people as if it were the last time you may have that opportunity.

Watch your words diligently. Words have great power to bless or to wound. When you speak carelessly or negatively, you damage others as well as yourself. This ability to verbalize is an awesome privilege, granted to humans created in God's image. You need help in wielding this mighty power responsibly. (Sara Young, *Jesus Calling: Enjoying Peace in His Presence*, August 3)

Though the world applauds quick-witted retorts, God's instructions about communication are quite different: Be quick to listen, slow to speak, and slow to become angry. Ask God to help you whenever you speak. If people are silent, pray before speaking to them. If people are talking, pray before responding. These are split-second prayers, but they put you in touch with God's presence. This way, your speaking comes under the control of God's spirit. As positive speech patterns replace your negative ones, the increase in your happiness will amaze you. (Sara Young, *Jesus Calling: Enjoying Peace in His Presence*, August 3)

Human words are powerful. Our tongues are small, but they are capable of wreaking great havoc. Any person who could perfectly control their words would be in perfect control of their entire bodies. Instead, as sinful human beings, our tongues are untamable. Our words are fire, igniting the entire course of our lives. Blessing God and cursing people should not come out of the same mouth. And yet, as fallen people, we do just that. We are corrupted. (bibleref.com, James 3:1–12)

CHOOSING TRUE HAPPINESS
～

What does it mean to be truly wise? True wisdom is not necessarily found in those with the most education, money, or friends. Rather, wise people can be spotted living wisely in humility, participating in good works, enjoying peace, singleness of purpose, and gentle lifestyles. (bibleref.com, James 3:1-12)

Nobody gets a free ride. Everybody has different challenges and obstacles to overcome during their lifetime. That's fine—it's all good. Struggle brings strength. Use those challenges and obstacles as incentives to keep moving forward. My *nonno*, my hero, would tell me, *"Va sempre avanti."* The message in Italian that he was teaching me was *always move forward*. When I'm faced with challenging circumstances in my life, I think about my grandfather's words of wisdom. Find strength through your challenges. Develop great character through your challenges. Live and learn through your challenges. Life is not about waiting for the storm to pass. It's about learning to sing, dance, and laugh in the rain. Start singing, dancing, and laughing right now. Your life is what you make of it. Don't make excuses and blame others for your mistakes or shortcomings. The potential of the human mind and body is immense. You can come out of the deepest, darkest holes if you keep pressing forward. Ultimately, you—and only you—are responsible for your life.

And nobody knows better how hard it is to press forward and keep going than Mason Sawyer. His life was shattered when his family was involved in a fatal car accident that took the lives of his brother Race Sawyer, his nephew Rider Sawyer, his wife Kortni. his son Riggins, and his daughter Franki. The accident occurred on July 25, 2021. Mason has now become solely focused on raising his son Blue, who survived the car accident. His mission is to help other people by living the 10/90 Principle. This principle of life being 10% what happens to you and 90% how you respond has inspired him to start a podcast named The10ninety. He has gone on to share his message as a public speaker. Please check out his podcast and website www.the10ninety.com. The name of his podcast and website come from the Lou Holtz quote: "Life is 10 percent what happens to you and 90 percent how you respond to it." Mason is a remarkable human being that has taught me about overcoming life's challenges. And no matter what happens in your life, you can still choose how to respond to any given circumstance. I find Mason's strength, positive attitude, and perseverance

I AGREE—IT'S UP TO ME...

very inspiring. It's absolutely extraordinary how he keeps going. Mason has highly motivated me to complete this book and helped me to make sure my life consists of happiness, purpose, and meaning. THANK YOU MASON, you are a wonderful human being! If you need motivation and purpose in your life, then look no further than to the life of Mason Sawyer.

Happiness is a choice that's attainable. You have to make a resolution to be happy. Be determined and persistent to achieve that happiness. True happiness lies within you. You must understand this and believe it.

Make a resolution to yourself to succeed. Be passionate about something. Be determined and persistent to succeed. Then go out there, take it, and make it happen. Believe in yourself, and others will believe in you. Whatever the mind of a person can perceive and believe, it can achieve. Visualize what you want, believe in what you want, and then just get it done. Where there's a will, there's a way.

I consider this section to be one of the most important parts in this book. The *I* is for you. Happiness all starts with you. Everything in life is a choice, including your happiness. Therefore, if you want to be truly happy, then it must be a major priority. Everything starts with our thinking. Your thoughts not only matter—they create matter.

What is one secret for true happiness in your life? To know who you really are. To know your true, unconditioned self. You are *being, awareness, spirit, soul,* and *bliss*.

Being is purely effortless awareness—literally—where you place your attention moment by moment. (2)

You can be present anywhere doing anything. The true source of peace and happiness exists inside us, beyond identifying with the mind. Beyond attachments and desires. Beyond being conditioned. All works of the egoic mind. You are the only person that can realize this is your *true self* (being, awareness, spirit, soul and bliss) Your true self cannot be known through thoughts and words. Your true self can be known only through experiencing it.

One way I stay in the present moment each day is by doing slow, deep, focused breathing. When you do deeper breathing, it increases oxygenation and can greatly enhance being. Just inhaling and exhaling can be a great experience. Challenge yourself to do slow, deep, focused breathing each and every day for at least five minutes per day. This can greatly enhance your level of calmness and relaxation. When doing it concentrate on listening to the sound of your breath or count. Practice having little or no thoughts. Do whatever it takes to stay in the present moment.

Give your full attention and awareness to your breath, the slow inhale, and, especially, the even-slower exhale, to live this present moment. When we slow ourselves down, specifically, our jump-all-over-theplace minds, all that remains is this moment of relaxed, aware being. It's amazing how accepting, relaxed, kind, and forgiving we can be in the present moment. (3) Develop a willingness to live and embrace being present in the moment.

True happiness already lies within all of us. This is your true self. Know your true self. Connect to your true self. Your true self emerges from a quiet mind. You can find true happiness from within. Start finding your inner peace now. It exists at this very moment. You have the power and control to tap into this happiness at any moment in your life. You can connect with that place of inner happiness within yourself. We have the power to switch on happiness whenever we want. The true reality of happiness is realizing that you can be happy whenever you want. You can achieve this because it is in you.

So, how do we do this? The answer is quite simple: Be, just be. Be present with little or no thought. That's the way to create blissfulness from within. Your duty is to be—*simply be*—not *be this or that*. Be still. Be silent. Be present, not knowing anything or becoming anything. The ego will disappear when you are still, and being will emerge. The mistake we make is identifying with the mind and listening and following its crazy and disturbing thoughts, which I call brain farts (lol). You are not your thoughts, and you are not your mind. Be as you really are (being, awareness). Discover that, and be happy and at peace. Silence the mind to sense your being in the present moment. You are awareness. Just give up being aware of other things that are of the false-self. Once you are able to do this, you will experience a very calm, relaxing, and peaceful feeling.

I AGREE—IT'S UP TO ME...

When the mind is absent, there will be perfect peace. Practice awareness in the present moment. Practice being present.

In Being, any other-ness, I-thought or "personal self" is absent. In Being, anxiety, depression, fear, and doubt naturally fade. To be calm, peaceful, completely engaged and fully relaxed reflects Being. Being is the space of the eternal response to true identity: "I AM." (4)

Be in the moment. Be present to what you are seeing, hearing, or doing. Just see, hear, and do, without any inner dialogue, without the voice in your head. The ultimate truth is so simple, it is nothing more than being in one's natural, original state, which is being, awareness, spirit, soul, and bliss.

The present moment is powerful. You have the ability to sense the aliveness of the present moment. You can sense your being and awareness in the present moment. This involves the discovery of yourself in the present. Sense the presence of the present. It's all about your journey into the now.

First, you need to be aware of the present moment. Our entire life consists of it. There has never been anything else. The only thing there ever was, ever is, and ever will be is the present moment. The "past" doesn't exist. You are thinking about the "past" in the present moment. The "future" doesn't exist. You are thinking about the "future" in the present moment. "Past" and "future" are thought about in the present moment.

Once you become aware of the present moment and realize that there is nothing else, then your journey into the present moment can begin. The key is to be—just be—with little or no thought. Present-moment awareness means thinking subsides, and something else arises that is primary, which is being, our true sense of self (I AM). The understanding of the self is the most important insight that any individual can have in life. Furthermore, it's imperative that you become aware of the spaces in between the thoughts. Once you become aware of the spaces in between the thoughts, your true sense of self, which is being, emerges. When this happens, it feels good and powerful.

How do you become aware of the present moment? Use your sense perceptions to slow down the overactive mind and/or take you out of thinking.

CHOOSING TRUE HAPPINESS

Do not let your being be absorbed by thinking. Use your sense perceptions without any negativity, judging, criticizing, labeling, naming, or enabling what you are perceiving. You want to be more rooted in the now, and then you are present. Use your sense perceptions to become aware of your environment. Just acknowledge what is. Appreciate what is. Feel the energy throughout your body. Feel the being and awareness of the present moment. (5)

What makes up the entirety of the present moment? Sense perceptions, thoughts (coming and going), feelings and spaces in between the thoughts. We associate ourselves with self-images, memories, experiences, expectations, sensations, attention, and intentions. (6)

How do we stay in the present moment and allow our true self, being, to emerge? Here are the things that help me to be present in the now:

* Prayer
* Slow, deep, focused breathing
* Meditating
* Looking at nature

You can learn to be present now. The true secret to happiness is to know who you really are and be, just be. Your duty is to be. The books and videos of Eckhart Tolle are a great place to begin. Personally, I want to send lots of love and appreciation to Eckhart for having such a positive impact on my life. Eckhart, thank you, thank you, thank you for sharing all of your valuable insights with the world and helping me to change my life.

Prayer

Prayer can move mountains. Prayer is extremely powerful. Don't worry about anything; instead, pray about everything. Continually communicate with God—on a daily basis. Tell God your needs, and thank him for all your blessings. Love God, serve God, talk to God, trust God, and thank God. I pray once in the morning and once at night.

I AGREE—IT'S UP TO ME . . .

Slow, Deep, Focused Breathing

Deep breathing is extremely relaxing. Deep breathing keeps us in the present moment. Deep breathing is a great anchor to the present moment. When done correctly, it can make you feel as though you are floating on a cloud. Deep breathing can be therapeutic and beneficial. Find a breathing technique that you like and works for you. Make it part of your everyday living. The deep-breathing technique I use is this: I take a slow, deep, and focused breath for as long as I can; I hold the breath for a few seconds. I breath out as slow and long as possible (listen to the sound of your breath when inhaling and exhaling). You can also add a positive affirmation, such as, *I am relaxed* or *I am calm*, after the deep breath. Make sure that, when you breathe in, your stomach goes out. Hold the breath for one to four seconds, and, then, when you breathe out, your stomach goes back in. Do this every day for at least 5 to 15 minutes. You should feel great and experience amazing results.

Meditating

Meditation is an opportunity to move into a dimension where there is no such thing as stress within you. It's a technique to guide you beyond negative thinking and slow down the busy mind. Meditating is a fantastic way to practice awareness and keep you in the present moment. When done daily and properly, meditating can give you a joyful feeling of floating on air. Be free from your thoughts, and remain in a state of meditation. I've used a meditation online, titled, "I Am Guided Meditation," which has worked well for me and lasts 23:20. It is like exercise for my mind. This meditation helps my mind expand in awareness and positivity.

Let meditation help your mind let go of thoughts, emotions, words, and actions that don't benefit you. Like all skills, the more you practice, the better you'll get at it. You don't need to reach enlightenment. Use meditation to rest your overactive brain. This way, you can feel rested and refreshed. Begin a meditation practice today.

CHOOSING TRUE HAPPINESS

There is an overwhelming amount of research showing how meditation changes the circuits in the part of the brain associated with contentment and happiness and stimulates the "feel-good" factor. (7)

Most of the time our mind is caught up in thoughts, emotions, and memories, and it's easy to fall into the grip of our ego's fears and demands. The imaginary ego is always after something, looking to get somewhere, and aiming to be someone. Ego stands at the ready to use anything to obtain some desire or another. Beyond this noisy internal dialogue is a state of pure being and awareness that is sometimes referred to as "the gap." This is the field of pure potentiality, which gives rise to everything that manifests in our physical universe. It is important to spend time each day silencing the mind and connecting to our essential nature: being, awareness, spirit, soul, and bliss.

One of the most powerful ways to enter this space of expanded consciousness is through a regular meditation practice. In meditation we experience our true self, which is pure awareness, pure potentiality, and pure being. When we're rooted in the experience of pure potentiality, our intentions can spontaneously manifest. Meditation takes us beyond the ego-mind into the silence and stillness of pure consciousness. This is the ideal state in which to plant our seeds of intention. (8)

As you learn to meditate, it will take time and practice to be able to "not think" for short intervals. Thoughts will eventually creep in; don't pay attention to those thoughts. Take a slow, deep, focused breath, and redirect your attention to the present moment. Listen carefully to the sound of your breath or count. Stay in the present moment, and allow the ego to dissolve. Free your egoic mind from the grip of the ego.

Looking at Nature

What is nature trying to tell us? Nature is trying to tell us that you can become one with God directly through nature. That is the true message of nature. Nature is God's way of communicating with us and showing us his presence,

I AGREE—IT'S UP TO ME...

power, and love. Every day, take time to look at trees, flowers, plants, animals, clouds, the sky, the sun, the moon, and the stars. Through nature—specifically, looking at a cloud—is how my spiritual awakening and journey occurred. Real spiritual awakening is when something emerges from within you that is deeper than who you thought you were.

What is the main hindrance that keeps us out of the present moment? It's our ego. When our egoic mind dominates, then we suffer. The ego wants to take away the only thing that really exists, which is the present moment. The ego wants to live in the "past" and "future." I will define ego as: identifying ourselves with our thoughts, feelings, beliefs, and memories, the *I* that we *think* we are, thriving on identification and separation (viewing ourselves as separate from everything else), struggling constantly to survive (the ego needs to raise itself up by bad-mouthing, discrediting, and putting down others,), seeing faults in others, complaining about others and situations (non-acceptance of what is). The ego needs to make itself great and superior both with people and situations. (*I'm right, and you are wrong*). It feeds on attachments (possessions, achievements) Watch for the 3 Cs of the Egoic Mind: Complaining, Criticizing, and Comparing.

Our natural state is true happiness, but our egoic mind wants to be in control and run the show. When the egoic mind dominates, big trouble will arise. The egoic mind tries to pull you in. The egoic mind likes to jump around from one thought, to another thought, to another thought ("monkey mind"). You should choose to slow down the egoic mind and control it, not follow it and destroy it. Don't follow the thought where it wants to take you, which is into another bigger thought, and then another bigger thought. It wants your attention and wants to grow and absorb your presence and being. When the egoic mind dominates, choose not to listen to that voice in your head. Choosing to follow negative thoughts can lead to more and bigger negative thoughts.

Before you know it, you have fallen into the trap of repetitive negative thinking, which is almost always focused on two areas—the past and the future. Avoid this trap at all costs. There's a tremendous amount of value in changing your negative thinking patterns. Thoughts can change, but not you (being, awareness). When you lose touch with your true self (being, awareness), thoughts afflict you, you see the world, and doubts arise, along with anxiety about the "future."

My egoic mind being in control was the cause of my anxiety. My many negative thoughts, mostly regarding my parents' divorce, kept going to the "past" and the "future," which don't exist. The "past" is gone. The "future" isn't here yet. Only the present moment, the now, exists. The only thing there is, ever was, and ever will be is the present moment. Which thoughts do you allow your mind to entertain?

"The only thing that is ultimately real about your journey is the step you are taking at this moment. That's all there ever is. Realize deeply that the present moment is all you ever have. Make the Now the primary focus of your life." (*The Power of Now*, Eckhart Tolle)

The egoic mind lives through "past" and "future." It identifies with the "past" and looks to the "future." The egoic mind overlooks the *Now* because it thinks "past" and "future" are more important. The fastest and best way to battle the egoic mind is to live in the present moment. Give more attention to the present moment, the *Now*. The ego cannot coexist with awareness. Acknowledging, accepting, and living in the present moment is the fastest and easiest way to say "Bye-bye" to the ego.

The present moment is crucial. Our entire life consists of the present moment. When you are present in the moment, the egoic mind can't survive; there's only being and awareness. Make friends with the present moment. Make the present moment the primary focus and factor in your life. What's your relationship with the present moment? The only place you are living from that is real is the here and now, the present moment. In this space is being, awareness, bliss, peace, clarity, and infinite spaciousness. Remember, you are existence itself. You are life itself. This is the very essence of who you are. May you experience the most profound moments of stillness and insight of the within. (Being, Awareness)

The following chart represents two ways of thinking. Use this chart to reflect on your thoughts.

I AGREE—IT'S UP TO ME . . .

Free Mind vs. Egoic Mind

FREE MIND	EGOIC MIND
Lives in the present moment	Lives in the past and future
Serves peace, happiness, and love	Causes, conflict, suffering, misery, and hatred
Manages your thoughts and emotions; you are in charge of your thoughts and emotions	Mismanages your thoughts and emotions; your thoughts and emotions are in charge of you
Quiet mind, less chatter	Busy mind, constant chatter
Just an observer of the voice in your head; no identification with thoughts, emotions, and reactions	Identifies with and believes the voice in your head (thoughts, emotions, and reactions) is you
Positive thinking, positive mindset	Negative thinking, negative mindset
Calm thinking; doesn't overthink	Restless mind; thinks too much
Doesn't identify with and follow irrational thoughts	Allows the ego to trick you through disguised thoughts or feelings
Aware of your negative thinking; knows it's just a ridiculous brain fart Doesn't allow the negative thinking to control you	Automatically pops up in your mind Wants you to believe and follow the negative thought, wants to pull you in and allow the negative thought to grow and keep growing
Solution-based thinking; is part of the solution	Problematic thinking; is part of the problem
Lowers stress levels, beneficial for mental health	Raises stress levels, detrimental for mental health
Makes good, smart choices	Makes poor, ineffective choices
Exhibits great self-control, including your wants and wishes Is content and satisfied	Exhibits poor self-control, including your wants and wishes Is never content and satisfied; always wants more and more
Compassionate toward yourself and others	Disapproving of yourself and others
Doesn't care about right and wrong	Always wants to be right, never wants to be wrong
Uses its attention and power in a positive way	Relentlessly pursues attention and power

CHOOSING TRUE HAPPINESS

FREE MIND	EGOIC MIND
Doesn't judge or criticize; makes a conscious choice to focus on the positive	Judges, criticizes, and labels people and things (especially as better than or worse than)
A healthy confidence in one's abilities, meekness	An arrogant confidence in one's abilities (exaggerated feelings of self-importance)
Doesn't take things personally, doesn't assume	Takes things personally, makes assumptions
Secure, peaceful, worry free	Insecure, fearful, worries
Patient	Impatient
Humble, reserved	Know-it-all
Equal to others in everyway	Superior to others
Accepts and learns from mistakes, makes changes	Can't accept your mistakes or others; doesn't learn from mistakes; keeps making the same mistakes over and over, doesn't change
Realizes human beings are awareness and being	Most of us don't realize its existence, yet we are under its influence
Serves a selfless society based on sharing and enjoying	Serves a selfish society based on greed, selfishness, dividing, and conquering
The benefit, best interests, and well-being of others guide and motivate what you think, feel, say, and do; what's good for others	The benefit, best interests, and well-being of yourself guide and motivate what you think, feel, say and do; what's good for me
Sees eternal life (infinite)	Sees only life on Earth

    Practice thinking using the free mind. Let your thinking be a source of love, respect, kindness, compassion, appreciation, strength, comfort, and direction. Have the courage to do the right thing. Avoid thinking with the egoic mind. Do not be blinded and tricked by your own thinking. Be what you are (Being, Awareness). That which is (Being, Awareness) is ever present. Even now you are it, and not apart from it (Being, Awareness). Be yourself (Being, Awareness) and nothing more. Think with the free mind, and let it guide how you feel, what you say, and what you do.

I AGREE—IT'S UP TO ME...

Freedom is about having fewer thoughts and thinking less. Freedom comes through learning how to balance thoughts and the present moment. Freedom comes as our life in thoughts diminishes and our experience of the present moment predominates. Freedom is being present. (9)

How you think, how you feel, what you say, and what you do, belong to either the Free Mind or the Egoic Mind.

The normal, natural state of all our minds is constantly busy. It chatters incessantly, bouncing from thought to thought, preparing for the future and reliving the past. We rarely stop to see the present. We often live in a revved-up state, in which we obsess over things we should have done or said. Similarly, we also constantly worry and plan for the future, so much so that we don't stop to notice the moment we are in right now. Missing the present moment means that you are missing your life. Missing your life equates to big-time unhappiness. If we don't learn to stop the robot-like, incessant racing of our minds, which renders us completely unconscious, these foggy moments can fill up most of our lives. Happiness cannot be found in future promises or past nostalgia. Happiness is right now! (10)

According to Tolle, identification with thinking gives rise to and maintains the ego, which is out of control. It believes it is real and tries hard to maintain its supremacy. Negative states of mind, such as anger, resentment, fear, envy, and jealousy, are products of the ego. When the ego is in control, these states of mind appear to us to be justified and also to be caused by some external factor. Usually, another person is blamed for these feelings. Their true cause, however, is not to be found in the content of your life, but in the very structure of the egoic mind. It needs enemies because it defines its identity through separation, and so it emphasizes the *other-ness* of others. For this reason, letting the ego be in control leads ultimately to violence, fighting, and war. This is madness, but the ego doesn't see it that way. (11)

Your mind is a wonderful tool. Allow it to be your best friend and not your worst enemy. You're in charge of your mind. You are the boss of your mind. Don't let your mind be in charge of you. It wants to be the boss—don't let it.

CHOOSING TRUE HAPPINESS

Beware, the mind is the master of all lies. Your mind can and will deceive you and do a number on you, but only if you allow it to. Remember that there's no cause, purpose, or reason behind strange and disturbing thoughts. I get these thoughts a lot every day. Your mind can be your best friend or worst enemy; the choice is yours. Train your brain or it will train you. Your mind should work like a mirror, showing you everything the way it is.

Our minds produce many thoughts each day. You need to be aware that your thoughts, feelings, and actions are all connected. Learn how your thoughts, feelings, and actions affect one another.

* Your thoughts lead to feelings and actions.
* Your feelings lead to thoughts and actions
* And your actions lead to feelings and thoughts

Automatic negative thoughts (ANT) are produced by the egoic mind. When these automatic negative thoughts enter your brain, you need to create a positive plan to deal with them. Here are some ideas:

* Recognize them
* Let them come and go
* Ignore them
* Realize your mind is lying to you
* Take a slow, deep, focused breath, and turn your attention inward.
* Take a slow, deep, focused breath, and, after slowly exhaling, say a positive affirmation. (*I am calm. I am relaxed.*)
* Use your sense of humor (laugh at them)
* Talk back to them
* Write it down right away; then immediately rip it up
* Replace a negative thought with a positive thought

I say to myself, "My egoic mind is creating brain farts" or "My brain is farting." Then, I usually laugh. Also, I replace the negative thought with a

I AGREE—IT'S UP TO ME...

positive, comforting thought such as, "God is real, and heaven exists." One of our greatest assets against stress is our ability to choose one thought over another. Don't let your egoic mind control your thoughts. Destroy the egoic mind, before it destroys you.

Negative thoughts release chemicals that make you feel sad and stressed. Do not focus on the negative thoughts. Your mind may try to keep taking you back to a negative thought. Don't follow it. Remember: Think bad, feel bad. Think good, feel good. How do you think?

According to Tolle, when the egoic mind is active and working, it will create a false sense of self. This false sense of self comes from habitual and repetitive thought patterns. Remember everything starts with your thinking. This false sense of self also comes from emotional and reactive patterns. It is important to let go of instinctive patterns such as judgmental reactions, anger, and jealousy. A false sense of self is not who you really are and will produce negative emotions. Who you really are is being, awareness, spirit, soul, and bliss. Our thoughts are like clouds that change and come and go, but we are like the sky—always present, always there, always existing.

Automatic positive thoughts (APT) are produced by the free mind. APT are the types of thoughts that we want to hear from the voice in our head. Positive thoughts release chemicals that help you feel calm and happy. Focus on these positive thoughts. Here are some ideas:

* Recognize them
* Pay attention to them
* Repeat them out loud
* Write them down (and then read them a few times daily)

If you choose to pay attention to certain thoughts, then choose to pay attention to the positive thoughts, not the negative thoughts. Remember: Think good, feel good. How do you think?

We all need to be aware that thinking can be an addiction. It is an addiction because it gives us a false sense of self. And people are unwilling to let this false sense of self go. Are you addicted to thinking? Does your mind not want to shut off? A good number of us are addicted to thinking, and many of us aren't even aware of it. Learn how to break your addiction to thinking. Practice sense perception without a need to label, name, or be judgmental. See—just see—without involving so much thinking and so many feelings. Just observe!

You see, our egoic minds want us to be addicted to thinking. And since the egoic mind is the master of all lies, it wants to constantly trick us and be in control. However, once you become aware of your mind, you are not identified with your mind anymore. A new dimension of awareness has come in. Not identifying with your mind allows our true self (Being, Awareness) to arise. The way out of excessive thinking is being present.

How do you give your mind a rest? The only time the mind can have a real rest is when it stops thinking and only experiences. How do you practice not-thinking? Become aware of your being in the present moment. Practice the state of not-thinking. Accept things as they are; be—just be.

Thoughts will come up and grab your full attention. This is what the mind does. Our priority is not to follow the thoughts. The thoughts are trying to pull us in and lead to more and more thoughts. In this case, just be an observer, and let go when you are thinking too much. Stay alert, observe, and feel, but be in the present moment. Staying in the present moment is the way to eliminate the suffering created through identifying with the mind.

According to Eckhart Tolle our lives have both an "inner purpose" and an "outer purpose." When it comes to meaning, one of the most important realizations is that your life has both an "inner purpose" and an "outer purpose." Tolle distinguishes between a primary purpose, which is your inner purpose and concerns Being, and a secondary purpose, which is your outer purpose and concerns doing. Tolle explains that "your inner purpose is to awaken." And awakening is the purpose shared by all humanity. On the other hand, he continues, "your outer purpose changes over time. Finding and living in

I AGREE—IT'S UP TO ME...

alignment with the inner purpose is the foundation for fulfilling your outer purpose. (12)

Our outer purpose changes with situations and necessarily involves time. Problems need time—that is to say past and future—to survive. Our inner purpose always remains the same, which is to be present in what we do. In awareness, there are no problems and no past or future. (13)

What Tolle is suggesting is that your inner purpose is not to be found in the outer world because "it does not concern what you do but who you are—that is to say, your state of consciousness."

Most important is the differentiation between Being and doing when it comes to purpose. Many people solely focus on their outer purpose, on the doing. But Tolle warns that, "outer purpose alone is always relative, unstable, and impermanent." In fact, he continues, "'Making it' in whatever field is only meaningful as long as there are thousands or millions of others who don't make it, so you need other human beings to 'fail' so that your life can have meaning." That's pretty intense. How can you separate meaning from comparison and live out your inner purpose? Tolle suggests that "the paradox is that the foundation for greatness is honoring the small things of the present moment instead of pursuing the idea of greatness. (14)

So awakening to your life's purpose is not to try to look to the future and expect fulfillment there, but to stay in the moment, allowing the ego to dissolve. Your life's inner purpose is primary, and your inner purpose is to awaken, to be conscious. Your inner purpose is to become more conscious. It's to live in the present moment. In whatever you do, your state of consciousness is the primary factor. (15)

Accomplish and fulfill your outer purpose while staying connected and focused on your inner purpose. Approach your outer purpose with full awareness. You will be happier on your journey and perhaps accomplish your desires, goals, and dreams faster. Find and connect to your inner purpose, and focus more on Being rather than doing.

"Not-thinking?" you might be asking. "Why would I want to do that?"

CHOOSING TRUE HAPPINESS

Of course, we need to think. If you and I weren't thinkers, I couldn't have written this book, and you wouldn't be able to read it. In addition, thinking about what happens in the "past" and the "future" is essential at times so that we can make wise decisions about our lives. No one wants to—or is able to—put an end to thinking.

That said, there are benefits to intentionally practicing what I call *not-thinking*.

Discursive thinking—the constant stream of one thought following another—is a deeply ingrained habit. It's so ingrained that we often start thinking just to occupy our minds. Many years ago, I remember going on vacation and saying to myself, "It will be great not to have to think about all the stresses at work." But it didn't take long for other stressful thoughts to rush in to fill that void.

It's an act of self-care to take a break from discursive thinking now and then, even during our waking hours. The practice of *not-thinking* is restful, calming, and restorative. In the words of Ayya Khema, one of my first Buddhist teachers:

"If we didn't give the body a rest at night, it wouldn't function very long. The only time the mind can have a real rest is when it stops thinking and only experiences. Once verbalization stops for a moment, not only is there quiet, but there is a feeling of contentment. That quiet, peaceful space is the mind's home. It can go home and relax just as we do after a day's work when we relax the body in an easy chair."

Here are three ways to practice *not-thinking*, followed by two tips to help you with the practice. All five are forms of mindfulness practice.

I hope you'll try these suggestions for a few minutes, several times a day; almost any time and any place will do. It takes practice because we're surprisingly addicted to discursive thinking.

1. **Open your five sense doors to whatever is happening around you.**

When you're lost in thought, it's easy to forget that there are five experiences available to you aside from analytical thinking. Those experiences

I AGREE—IT'S UP TO ME...

are: what you're seeing, hearing, smelling, tasting, and feeling physically. Let your attention rest on whatever sensory input is most predominant at the moment. It might be the sight of an art print on the wall. It might be the murmur of a conversation nearby. It might be the smell and taste of an apple you're eating. It might be the physical sensation on your skin of the clothes you're wearing.

When you try this, if you drift back into discursive thinking, simply note it without aversion or judgment and return your attention to what's going on at the five sense doors.

As you become skilled at this practice, you can get bold and instruct your mind to stop thinking by trying a practice I call "Drop It" in my books. In short, when you notice that your mind is caught up in thoughts, gently but firmly say, "Drop It." Then immediately direct your attention to what is happening right around you.

As an alternative to resting your attention on what is most predominant in your experience, you could try the more structured practice I wrote about in "Five Minutes of Mindfulness Magic." In that piece, you'll find an exercise that guides your awareness systematically from one sensory experience to another.

Left unattended, the mind tends to dwell on thoughts about the past and the future. But if you consciously put your attention on the many sensory inputs all around you, you can take yourself out of discursive-thinking mode. This is relaxing and renewing on a deep level.

2. **Open the hand of thought.**

Zen teacher Kosho Uchiyama wrote a book called *Opening the Hand of Thought*. I use this phrase to practice *not-thinking*. When I realize I'm lost in unproductive discursive thinking, I'll open my hand and lightly blow on my palm as if I'm dispersing the thoughts into the air like dandelion seeds. I imagine all my trivial concerns and opinions blowing out of my mind, leaving me free to experience the world without the burden of analyzing every moment of my experience. When I do this, I can feel

CHOOSING TRUE HAPPINESS

my mind relax and, just like Ayya Khema said would happen, a feeling of contentment arises.

3. **Let the world speak for itself.**

I learned this from the Tibetan Buddhist teacher Pema Chödrön. She practices "letting the world speak for itself" when she's in places like airports, where she has a wait ahead of her. Instead of picking up something to read or getting lost in thoughts about the past and the future, she just sits and watches what's going on around her.

When I find myself in a waiting room, instead of giving in to that ingrained habit of picking up a magazine, I consciously practice *not-thinking* by opening my five senses and taking in what's happening around me. As I do this, I say to myself, "Let the world speak for itself." Not only does this provide welcome relief from thinking, but I've discovered that a world-that-speaks-for-itself is almost always a fascinating place.

Two tips for successfully practicing *not-thinking*:

1. **Don't let thoughts "stick."**

As you're practicing not-thinking, an unpleasant thought might arise. Thoughts—particularly unpleasant ones—tend to stick like glue. More often than not, this leads you to spin the thought out into elaborate and stressful stories about the past or the future—stories that have little or no basis in fact. The Buddha called this tendency *papanca*, which translates as "proliferation of thoughts."

Here's an example. You've consciously put your attention on all the sights around you. As you're doing this, the thought arises, "I don't feel well." You could stop the thinking process right there and treat "I don't feel well" as nothing more than a factual description of how you feel at the moment.

Instead, soon you're off on what I think of as the equivalent of a guitar riff. You take that simple "theme"—"I don't feel well"—and the riff begins: "I'm going to have a horrible day"; "Nothing will go right"; "I may never feel well again." Soon, the fact that you don't feel well has colored everything about your day, making you miserable emotionally.

I AGREE—IT'S UP TO ME...

Consider, though, these words from the Platform Sutra of the Seventh Century Chinese Chan (Zen) master, Hui Neng:

"No-thought" is to see and to know all things with a mind free from attachment. When in use, it pervades everywhere, yet it sticks nowhere.

Hui Neng is not saying that you'll always be able to empty your mind of thoughts. Rather, he's suggesting that when a thought does arise—such as "I don't feel well"—you try to respond to it without attachment, which means simply watching it until it passes out of your mind in the same way that the sound of a bird singing arises and then passes out of your mind. When thoughts "stick nowhere," to use his words, you don't go down that *papanca* road, spinning a simple, fact-based thought out into every stressful scenario you can come up with.

The Vietnamese monk and teacher Thich Nhat Hanh describes "not sticking" this way: "Thoughts and feelings come and go like clouds on a windy day." I like to keep his phrase in mind when I practice *not-thinking*.

2. **Let go of opinions and judgments.**

It's easier to practice *not-thinking* if you put aside opinions and judgments. Doing this also brings welcome relief from constantly passing judgment on everything around you. Most of us immediately form opinions about our environment (too hot, too cold) and about people (too talkative, too quiet). Listening to this running commentary is stressful and exhausting. When the Thai Buddhist monk, Ajahn Chah, was asked what the greatest obstacle for his students was, he replied, "Opinions." When you're able to let go of opinions and judgments, you're letting go of a big chunk of what's going on in your mind.

Discursive thinking is a deeply ingrained habit, but there's no reason to be distressed about this. "Thinking" is what minds do. These suggestions are intended to help you give your mind a rest for a few minutes throughout the day. Consciously placing your attention—without commentary—on what's going on around you is restful, calming, and restorative.

Happy *not-thinking*!

© 2015 Toni Bernhard. (16)

CHOOSING TRUE HAPPINESS

Through my experiences, I've found the practice of *not-thinking* to be restful, calming, rejuvenating, and restorative. Slow, deep, focused breathing and looking at nature works for me.

Pleeeeease do not look to the mind to provide you with your sense of identity. Our human minds are trained to give opinions and pass judgment. We often are sorting and classifying things through a good/bad lens. See things as they are. Don't see things through the eyes of a critical, lying, sneaky, and convincing mind.

The craziness is caused by thinking without awareness. The ego is able to keep us in its grip when we are thinking without awareness. What can happen when the ego has us in its grip? We suffer. We create sufferings in our mind such as fear, frustration, anger, resentment, jealousy, anxiety, sadness, and stress. Much of the suffering we create for ourselves is because of our identification with our thoughts and with our sense of self. However, if you take charge of your mind, you can create a state of great happiness and pure bliss. Every day I face the challenge of being in charge of my thoughts and emotions. I strive to win most of the days.

Awareness (Enlightenment) is the ego's ultimate disappointment. When you are continually aware and present, you become enlightened, and the ego can't survive. Challenge yourself, and see how much of the day you can spend in Being and Awareness. Instead of your ego constantly dominating you, dominate your ego. You may be in a constant struggle against your ego, however, you do have the power and ability to dominate your ego.

Our free mind and egoic mind can be extremely powerful. Use the chart (see above), "Free vs. Egoic Mind," to reflect on your thoughts. What will you exercise and practice? What will you choose to see, use, follow, identify with, and react to? Which mind does your thinking serve: the free mind or the egoic mind? Do you want to be the master of your mind, or do you want your mind to be the master of you? Do you want to be in charge of your mind, or do you want your mind to be in charge of you? Think with the free mind and let it guide how you feel, what you say, and what you do.

I AGREE—IT'S UP TO ME . . .

"The biggest issue with human beings is they do not know how to handle their thoughts and emotions."
—S<small>ADHGURU</small> (17)

"Accept—then act. Whatever the present moment contains, accept it as if you had chosen it. Always work with it, not against it. Make it your friend, not your enemy. This will miraculously transform your whole life."
—E<small>CKHART</small> T<small>OLLE</small> (18)

"Passion is what makes life interesting, what ignites our soul, fuels our love and carries our friendships, stimulates our intellect, and pushes our limits."
—P<small>AT</small> T<small>ILLMAN</small> (19)

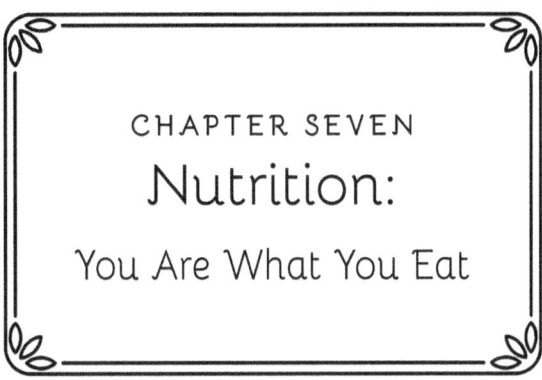

CHAPTER SEVEN

Nutrition:

You Are What You Eat

"Our food should be our medicine, and
our medicine should be our food."
—Hippocrates (1)

We've all heard the expression "You are what you eat." Well, it's true for the most part. Eat healthy foods and drink healthy drinks, and you should feel good. Eat unhealthy foods and drink unhealthy drinks, and you probably won't feel good. Eating and drinking good will help you feel good. Eating and drinking bad will help you feel bad. The way you think, feel, and act is connected to what you eat and drink.

What's the first step in improving your health through nutrition? Well, it involves the basic element needed for all living things to survive. Water. Yes, water. Water is crucial for your well-being, survival, and overall health.

Water is involved in many vital functions that our bodies perform on a daily basis. An average adult body is about 50 to 65 percent water. A woman's body is about 50 to 60 percent water. An infant's body is amazingly about 70 percent water. Furthermore, water is involved in making up our tissues, organs, fluids, and bones. The following are estimates of the percentage of water:

* Brain 75%
* Heart 75%
* Lungs 86%
* Muscles 75%
* Liver 85%
* Kidney 83%
* Bones 22%
* Blood 83%
* Saliva 95%
* Perspiration 95%

The percentage of water in our bodies is affected by our body weight and our fat percentage. Also, keep in mind that the amount of water in your body progressively decreases from birth to old age.

So how much water should you drink? The amount of water you should be drinking on a daily basis depends on your body weight. You should be drinking half your body weight in pounds in ounces. For example, if you weigh 150 pounds, you should drink 75 ounces of water daily. The single most important thing you can do for your health through nutrition is drink the right amount of water every day. Drink a lot of water. Make sure the water you drink is free of all chemicals and contaminants. You might be asking yourself, "How am I going to drink all that water every day?" Here are a couple of suggestions.

You can break it down by the hour. Let's say you weigh 160 pounds. Therefore, you need to drink 80 ounces of water daily. Let's use an 8-hour period, say 10 a.m. to 6 p.m. Therefore, you need to drink 10 ounces of water every hour during the 8-hour period.

Here's another way you can do it. Let's say you weigh 150 pounds. Therefore, you need to drink 75 ounces of water daily. Let's use our three basic daily meals—breakfast, lunch, and dinner. Therefore, you need to drink 25 ounces

NUTRITION: YOU ARE WHAT YOU EAT

of water at each meal. These are just a couple of suggestions. You can use any technique that works for you. Just do it and drink that water.

For those of you who don't like water, a healthy alternative to water is lemon water. Lemon water has a numerous amount of health benefits. Simply take a fresh whole lemon and make lemon juice; then add the juice to the water. It only takes a minute, and your mind and body will be thanking you if you drink lemon water on a daily basis. Make sure to use a straw when drinking lemon water. If you don't like the flavor of lemon, then find another healthy and natural alternative to add to your water. Just make sure you are drinking enough water every day.

Many nutrition and dietary experts suggest we eat five to nine servings of fruits and vegetables every day. The USDA has stated that one-half cup is a serving size. I usually follow the daily suggested servings of fruits and vegetables. In addition, I stick with a minimal sugar, low-carb (exception: healthy carbs), high-protein diet.

Those five to nine servings are combined, so, for example, you may eat two cups of fruits and two cups of vegetables daily, providing you with eight servings. Children need at least three servings of vegetables and two servings of fruit daily. A great way to eat the right amount of fruits and vegetables is to incorporate them into your daily routine. A lot of people make it their business to drink their coffee in the morning. It becomes a routine. It becomes a habit. Well, make it your business to eat fresh fruits and vegetables daily. Make it a daily routine. Make it a daily habit. You will feel great and perhaps increase your chances of living longer. Do you want to feel great? Do you want to live longer? Isn't that enough incentive to eat fresh fruits and vegetables? Eat healthy, fresh foods, and feel refreshed and healthy. The way you eat and drink strongly impacts your physical and mental health and the way you think, feel, and experience life.

ABCs of Nutrition

A—Asparagus, Avocados, Almonds, Apples, Acai Berries, Anchovies

B—Broccoli, Blueberries, Beets, Bananas, Barley, Broccoli Sprouts, Blackberries, Black Beans, Bran Flakes, Brown Rice, Brussel Sprouts, Bok Choy, Beef

CHOOSING TRUE HAPPINESS

C—Cherries, Cinnamon, Cauliflower, Carrots, Cranberries, Celery, Collard Greens, Cabbage, Cantaloupes, Chicken
D—Dates, Dill, Dandelion Greens, Dark Chocolate
E—Edamame, Elderberries, Eggplant, Endive, Eggs
F—Fish Oil, Figs, Fava Beans
G—Garlic, Grapes, Ginger, Grapefruits, Goji Berries, Ginseng Root
H—Honey (Raw, Organic), Horseradish, Herring
I—Inca Berries, Iceberg Lettuce
J—Jalapeños
K—Kiwi, Kale, Kidney Beans, Kippers
L—Lemons, Lentils, Leeks, Lettuce, Lemongrass, Lima Beans
M—Mushrooms, Milk (Almond and Soy), Mangoes, Mackerel
N—Nuts, Nectarines
O—Onions (Red), Oats, Olives, Oranges, Oil (Avocado & Olive)
P—Pomegranates, Peas, Peppers (Red), Pumpkin, Prunes, Papayas, Peaches, Pears, Pineapples
Q—Quinoa
R—Radish, Raspberries, Rhubarb, Red Wine
S—Spinach, Seeds (Chia, Flax, Hemp, Pumpkin, Sunflower), Sweet Potatoes, Salmon (Wild), Strawberries, Scallops, Swiss Chard, Sardines, Scallions, Squash, Spirulina, Sumac
T—Tea (Matcha Green), Turmeric, Tomatoes, Tofu, Trout, Turnip, Tuna (Wild), Turkey
U—Uncooked Vegetables
V—Various Colors of Vegetables, Vinegar (Apple Cider)
W—Water, Wheatgrass, Walnuts, Wasabi, Watermelon, Watercress, Winter Squash
X—X Out Sugar
Y—Yams, Yogurt (Non-Fat Greek)
Z—Zucchini

NUTRITION: YOU ARE WHAT YOU EAT

People who take time to chew slowly have better digestion and feel fuller, faster. Being a slower eater might help your waistline and body mass index.

Eat a healthy, balanced diet. Think about your selection and moderation when choosing what you eat and how much you eat. I try to stick to a whole-food, plant-based diet. Choose to be healthy by drinking enough water and eating the right amounts of fruits and vegetables.

What do I use often to benefit my overall health?[6]

1. Water
2. One large lemon squeezed in 16 ounces of water. Make sure you use a straw to drink the lemon water.
3. Kiwi
4. Organic blueberries (1 cup)
5. Banana
6. Walnuts (1/4 cup)
7. Almonds (1/4 cup)
8. Hemp Seeds
9. Organic Chia Seeds
10. Matcha Green Tea Powder with organic raw honey
11. Avocado
12. One glass of red wine
13. 5 to 9 daily servings of fruits and vegetables
14. Supplements Used:
    a. Red Yeast Rice
    b. Cinnamon Bark Extract
    c. Fish Oil
    d. Turmeric
    e. Organic Mushroom Extract Powder
    f. Coenzyme Q10

---

[6] Use moderation and consult with your doctor when consuming anything on this list. Also, when taking any supplements please follow all directions on the label and consume only as directed.

CHOOSING TRUE HAPPINESS

g. Vitamins C, D, and E
h. Psyllium Husk
i. Ashwagandha
j. Beet Root Powder
k. Immune System Supplement
l. Lemon Balm
m. Passion Flower
n. Chamomile
o. Multivitamin
p. Garlic Extract
q. Green Tea Extract
r. Magnesium
s. Calcium

"Water is the most neglected nutrient in your diet, but one of the most vital."
—JULIA CHILD (2)

"Don't dig your grave with your own knife and fork."
—ENGLISH PROVERB (3)

"An ounce of prevention is worth a pound of cure."
—BENJAMIN FRANKLIN (4)

CHAPTER EIGHT
Good Sense of Humor:
Just Laugh

"Laughter is an instant vacation."
—MILTON BERLE (1)

I will define laughter as: an expression or appearance of merriment or amusement; finding pleasure in something.[7]

Have you ever heard the expression, "Laughter is the best medicine" or "Laughter is the music of the soul"? Well, these expressions are true. Laughter is great for you and can trigger joy and provide great happiness. In addition, laughter is very good for your mental health, and it's free. We should all laugh on a daily basis. In fact, a day in your life should not pass by without including laughter in it. Laugh daily! It's very important to always keep a good sense of humor throughout your lifetime. Laughter can bring about positive emotions and help keep you feeling better and younger. Take it with you wherever you go, and be ready to use it as often as possible. There are many situations that can be dealt with appropriately and effectively with a good sense of humor and

---
7 www.dictionary.com

some laughter. Laughter can take the place of negative emotions such as anger, jealousy, guilt, and resentment, all of which can create harmful chemicals that may affect your happiness level.

Next time you feel like you are going to get mad, laugh instead. Laugh the loudest when the joke is on you. Laughter is much healthier than these negative emotions, and your body will be releasing chemicals that are good for you. Laughter can help resolve conflicts and de-escalate situations.

Laughter is powerful. A good sense of humor might be your best ally when you encounter certain situations in your life. During challenging times, it's easy to lose your sense of humor and get caught up in these times. Please don't allow this to happen. Using your sense of humor may bring light and acceptance to the situation and help you cope with it. Personally speaking, keeping and using my sense of humor is definitely one thing that has helped me through challenging times. I try not to let one day go by without laughing. Try to find the humor in as many things as possible. You might surprise yourself with how many things a good sense of humor can improve.

Never lose touch with that little kid in you—the kid who giggles and goes hysterical over silly little things. Whenever possible, be a kid at heart, and laugh, laugh—and then laugh some more. There are a lot of things that adults can learn from children, and laughter is definitely one of them. A fun little boy or fun little girl is inside every man and woman. We just need to search inside ourselves. Once you find it, tap into it and use it. Don't be embarrassed. Be proud that you haven't lost touch with the little kid in you. It's that innocent, care-free, fun personality that will help you in being happy. I will never lose touch with the little kid in me.

Stop taking things so seriously. A lot of those things are petty anyway, in the whole scheme of life. So, why stress it? It's not worth it. Often, situations are not as "bad" as we make them out to be. So, just laugh, and don't be afraid or embarrassed. It's perfectly fine to have a laughing fit and make a scene. Remember this has a lot to do with your perspective and how you respond to stressful events. Our mind tries to convince us that life is serious. However, life isn't as serious as our mind tries to make it.

GOOD SENSE OF HUMOR: JUST LAUGH

I myself am a huge jokester. I've noticed that my daughters Isabella and Olivia have a great sense of humor and laugh often. I'm thrilled to see that my daughters have my sense of humor. We think that a lot of things are funny. We are constantly joking around and being silly. If you are not sure how to incorporate more of a sense of humor into your life, then learn how. Find humor in your life. Being a jokester comes very natural to me, however, it doesn't come as natural for everybody.

Research has shown that laughter has a wide range of health benefits. Laughter can help you with stress management. Yes, laughter leads to less stress. It accomplishes this by reducing the level of stress hormones and increasing the level of hormones such as neurotransmitters and endorphins. Laughter will definitely help you with the physical effects of stress.

Laughter can help your immune system. Yes, that's right: Laughter can increase your immunity by increasing the number of antibody-producing cells. Laughter also enhances the effectiveness of T cells. Try laughing more, and perhaps you will get sick less often.

Laughter provides a physical release and an emotional release. It's a great outlet. Have you ever said to yourself, "I don't know whether I should laugh or cry"? Well, choose laughing—it's very good for you. Furthermore, laughing contracts the abs, can exercise the diaphragm, and works out the shoulders, leaving the muscles more relaxed afterward. It can even provide a good workout for your heart. Have you ever laughed so hard that you couldn't breathe?

Laughter is contagious. I know once I start cracking up, my daughters get in on it, and vice-versa. Laughter connects us. It improves the quality of our life and our relationships. Why not improve the quality of your life and relationships with laughter? And if you are married, I know that you can definitely use some laughter in your marriage. Laugh together—it's much healthier for the relationship than bickering, arguing, or fighting. Think about it: Most things that you bicker, argue, and fight about are petty. When this is happening, ask yourself, "Will this matter in an hour, a day, a week, a month, or a year" Most of the time, the answer will be "No."

CHOOSING TRUE HAPPINESS

Humor is a character strength. As humans, humor allows us to experience something beneficial we have in common. There's nothing like sharing a good laugh with someone. We must always remember we have far more similarities than differences.

The focal point really needs to be on our similarities, not on our differences. We may look different on the outside, but on the inside, we are all the same. There's no such thing as "normal" or "abnormal," "able" or "disabled"; we are all equal. Therefore, we all should be treated equally. Your ethnicity, how you look, your weight, your height, and your religion shouldn't matter. We are all part of one race, the human race. We are all God's Children, part of one family, God's family. If only everyone realized this and treated one another as family, the world would be a beautiful place.

Laughter is free and convenient, and can be used anytime and anywhere. Be sure to have your sense of humor always readily available to be used. Using your sense of humor helps us coexist peacefully with others.

You might be thinking to yourself, *How can I incorporate more laughter into my life?* Here are some ways you can get more laughter into your life:

* **Television:** (comedy, reality, and prank shows like "Impractical Jokers") Also, I love Sebastian Maniscalco, Anthony Rodia, Chris Rock, and Eddie Murphy
* **Movies:** (comedies)
* **Hanging out** with friends (perhaps a regular game night)
* **Comedy clubs:** Watch and listen to comedians
* **Tell jokes**
* **Be in the now**
* **If you have kids, play with them**
* **Go roller skating** (especially if you've never tried it before)
* **Play with a pet**
* **Sing and dance** (Sometimes after dinner, I put my radio on and dance wild and crazy with my daughters, and sometimes even my wife)

GOOD SENSE OF HUMOR: JUST LAUGH

* **Listen to radio stations** doing their prank phone calls (I listen to "The Elvis Duran Morning Show" on Z100. I love their phone tap)
* **Play innocent and fun pranks on people**
* **Focus on maintaining a sense of humor** (This may require a shift in attitude, which is fine, because an attitude adjustment never hurt anyone)
* Last and definitely not least, try **laughing at yourself**

Be a jokester. It's great for your health. And to all those serious people who hardly laugh, lighten up, and start laughing. Life is too short. You might want to remind those "proper" and "serious" people that laughter is the best medicine and the music of the soul. Take every opportunity to appropriately joke with and tease your family, friends, colleagues, neighbors, and anybody else you might want to laugh with.

Make laughing part of your daily life. Laugh often, so it becomes a routine or habit. Make it happen. I try to laugh every day. Laughing has numerous overall health benefits. Laughing can bring you and others around you greater happiness. When was the last time you had a really good laugh?

> "A good laugh heals a lot of hurts."
> —Madeleine L'Engle (2)

> "As soon as you have made a thought, laugh at it."
> —Lao Tzu (3)

> "I never would have made it if I could not have laughed. It lifted me momentarily out of this horrible situation, just enough to make it livable."
> —Viktor Frankl (4)

CHAPTER NINE
Help Often
and You Shall Receive

"Every word you utter, every action you take in your life—is it for everyone's well-being, or is it just about you? Just fix this one thing."

—Sadhguru (1)

I will define *helping as aiding*, improving, promoting, and giving assistance and relief.[8]

Make it easier for (someone) to do something by offering one's services or resources. Improve (a situation or problem); be of benefit to. Assist (someone) to move in a specified direction.[9]

When was the last time you helped somebody or a situation? Hopefully, not that long ago. Helping people and situations makes you feel good. So why not do it often? That way, you can feel good often. Do kind acts, and say nice things. You'll be amazed how it comes back to you—karma is real. Help situations and people often. Remember, to give is to receive. Therefore,

---

8 https://www.merriam-webster.com
9 Google's English dictionary, provided by Oxford Languages

CHOOSING TRUE HAPPINESS

it is better to give than to receive. The person who serves the best profits the most. Lose yourself in the service of others. The way to truly rise is by lifting others, not controlling and conquering others. There is no greater fulfillment than to touch and transform lives. Your happiness level will increase the more you show that you care for the happiness of others.

Performing acts of kindness can have powerful effects on our overall well-being and happiness. I love to do random acts of kindness. I look for opportunities and make it a point to do loving, kind, caring, and generous things for others. I am my happiest when I'm helping others or a situation. God has given me the motivation, tools, and natural abilities to help others. Be good to as many people as possible. Be helpful in as many situations as possible. Kindness matters and makes a difference. An act of kindness can turn someone's life around for the better.

A sense of duty and purpose outside ourselves is very important for our overall happiness level. Create meaning and purpose in your life that involves helping others and situations. Find ways to be generous with your love, time, care, and money. Have a strong desire to help those who are in need. Connect to a wider purpose, and devote yourself to the well-being of others, and you will help yourself thrive. Make the change from a "me" mentality to a "we" mentality. Be selfless, and have a "we" mentality.

Do good things and feel good. Believe and trust good things will come back to you. Do bad things, and you'll feel bad. Believe and trust that bad things will come back to you. I strongly believe in karma. When you do good things, you live with a clear head, and you feel better about yourself. When you do bad things, you don't live with a clear head, and your conscience will catch up with you sooner or later. Personally, the more I do, the better I feel; the less I do, the worse I feel.

Remember that your words and actions have a strong effect on other people. Our fingerprints never fade from the lives that we touch. Some people don't realize how their words and actions impact the lives of others. Try to consistently make a positive impact on the lives of others. You never know how you can turn someone else's life around by what you say to them or do for them.

HELP OFTEN, AND YOU SHALL RECEIVE

Everyone you come across has challenges in their lives, so be kind to them. Everyone has a me, too story. Also, keep in mind that the person everybody likes is the person who generally likes everybody. Therefore, if a lot of people like you, then you probably like a lot of people. If a lot of people don't like you, then, chances are, you probably don't like a lot of people.

Why does it take a crisis or tragedy for people to come together and help one another? Why can't we just help one another on a regular basis under ordinary circumstances? Imagine what it would be like if everyone helped someone often.

Remember: Everybody has feelings. And people don't forget how you made them feel. So, try as much as possible to treat others the way you like to be treated (Golden Rule). Kindness and respect are a language we all understand. Most people respond to respect and kindness. It is much more effective to treat people with kindness and respect than to treat them with unkindness and disrespect. Mistreating people won't get you anywhere, except into trouble. No act of kindness is ever too small. Kindness is powerful and contagious. Kindness changes everything! Let kindness be your superpower.

Imagine all the money, time, effort, energy, thought power, and strategy put into war. Now take all that, and put it into helping one another and caring for each other. What an amazing world we would live in! Be the peace you want to see in others. Be the peace you want to see in the world. Pray every day for world peace.

One way you can help others is by donating items. A lot of us have accumulated excess "stuff." This is a perfect opportunity to reduce clutter and help others by donating. On several occasions, my wife and I have donated many items from our home.

Let helping people and situations be part of who you are. Eventually, it will happen if you are consistent and determined. Let helping become part of your nature; that way, it will happen naturally. This will be beneficial to all involved. When you help others, you help yourself.

True success in life is not measured by the kind of car you drive, the type of house you live in, how much money or materialistic items you have, or the

CHOOSING TRUE HAPPINESS

brand of clothes that you wear. True success is determined by how your life has impacted and affected the lives of others. Experience the immense fulfillment of touching people's lives in a positive and deep way.

Start immediately helping people and situations on a daily basis. Create and look for opportunities to help situations and people often. You will reap the benefits and increase your chances of living a happier life. Who are you going to help? What situation are you going to improve?

> "Unexpected kindness is the most powerful, least costly, and most underrated agent of human change."
> —Bob Kerry (2)

> "Kindness is not an act. It is a lifestyle."
> —Anthony Douglas (3)

> "The surest way to be happy is to seek happiness for others."
> —Martin Luther King, Jr. (4)

CHAPTER TEN
Exercise Is the Key:
Just Do It

"When it comes to health and well-being, regular exercise is about as close to a magic potion as you can get."
—Tich Nhat Hanh (1)

I will define exercise as *an activity* that requires physical or mental exertion, especially when performed to develop or maintain fitness.[10]

The benefits of exercise are endless. It contributes to your overall well-being. It's great for your physical and mental health. It's a fantastic outlet for stress and an exceptionally effective way to combat stress. You will feel better, have more energy, and maybe even live longer. Exercising might even become an addiction for you.

Be proactive! Choose activities that you like and are fun. Even brisk walking 30 to 45 minutes, three or four times a week is great for you. Just pick yourself up and do it—stop making excuses. Excuses will not get you anywhere. Exercise, exercise, exercise!

---

10 www.thefreedictionary.com

Exercising is one of the best things you can do for yourself. Exercise can help you with weight management. It can help you lose weight and/or maintain your weight. When you exercise, you burn calories. The more intense the physical activity, the more calories you burn. You may also feel better about your appearance and yourself when you exercise often. Exercise can boost your confidence and improve your self-esteem and self-concept. People who are content with their weight have a tendency to be confident with their self-esteem and self-concept.

Exercise can help prevent illnesses and diseases. It gets the blood pumping and flowing smoothly. Exercise can decrease your risk of cardiovascular diseases by elevating your good cholesterol and decreasing your triglycerides. It can help you manage or even prevent arthritis, strokes, type 2 diabetes, and certain types of cancer.

Exercise can improve your mental health. It can give you an emotional lift and improve your mood. Exercise can help you prevent or manage anxiety and depression. It is a fantastic outlet and is therapeutic. Exercise is the best drug. It can stimulate various brain chemicals, such as endorphins and serotonin, that may leave you feeling happier and more relaxed. Personally, when I exercise a few times a week, very little bothers me. I'm usually in a great mood and rarely feel stressed. Exercise is the key for me.

Exercising can give you more energy. It can improve your muscle strength and increase your endurance. Exercising and being physically active delivers oxygen and nutrients to your tissues and helps your cardiovascular system work more efficiently. You will have more energy to go about your day if your heart and lungs are working more efficiently.

Exercise may help you sleep better. Consistent exercising might help you fall asleep faster and deepen your sleep. Be careful not to exercise close to bedtime, because you might have too much energy to fall asleep.

Exercising can be fun. Find physical activities that you enjoy. Play sports, take a zumba or yoga class, take self-defense courses, or try jump-roping. Go walking, biking, hiking, swimming, dancing, or gardening. Not only does exercising benefit your physical and mental health, but

EXERCISE IS THE KEY: JUST DO IT

being physically active may help you connect with friends, family, and other people.

Let exercise be a part of your life as you grow older. You can still choose to live a very active lifestyle in your golden years. Age is just a number. You're only as old as you think and feel. Here's my plan:

Do not let the old man in. Once he's in, he doesn't want to leave.

A body in motion tends to stay in motion. A body at rest tends to stay at rest. So, get up and kick it into gear. Exercising will improve your quality of life. Exercise and physical activity can transform your life in ways that you never thought were possible. How do you take care of your body? What type of exercises do you incorporate in your life?

> "Movement is a medicine for creating change in a person's physical, emotional, and mental states."
> —CAROL WELCH (2)

> "To keep the body in good health is a duty, for, otherwise, we shall not be able to trim the lamp of wisdom, and keep our mind strong and clear."
> —GAUTAMA BUDDHA (3)

> "Physical activity is an excellent stress-buster and provides other health benefits as well. It also can improve your mood and self-image."
> —JON WICKHAM (4)

CHAPTER ELEVEN
Love, Love, Love

"Love is the most powerful force in the universe, a want and
need that connects every human being on the planet."
—Scarlett Lewis (1)

I *will define* love *as: "an intense feeling of deep affection"; "a great interest
and pleasure in something"; "a person or thing that one loves."*[11]

It all starts with self-love. If you want to live a healthy, happy, love-giving life, then it all starts with loving yourself first. It's difficult to love others if you first don't show love to yourself. You should strive to love yourself the way God loves you. God created you in his image, so there's definitely something to love.

Love is one of the most powerful emotions of all. Love is very powerful and can conquer many things. Love is all-consuming, empowering; love lives in each of us. As Lao Tzu said, "Love is of all passions the strongest, for it attacks simultaneously the head, the heart, and the senses." People who have a lot of

---

11 https://www.fitzmuseum.cam.ac.uk/gallery/hiddenhistories/theme/love.html

love in their lives are much happier and healthier than those who do not. Every human being has the need to love and be loved. This need is as important as the air that we breathe, the water that we drink, and the food that we eat. If one is to be truly happy, the need to love and be loved is a necessity. Choose to love without limits and welcome love into your life with open arms. Love can create amazing events and bring out the best in people. As a matter of fact, many people in the world are products of love!

When you have a lot of love in your life, the benefits are numerous. It gives you the chance to care for other people and to be cared for. Love gives you the opportunity to laugh, dance, share, hug, and sing. It provides direction and excitement in your life. It gives you strength, courage, support, determination, persistence, and perseverance. Love gives you hope and fulfills your dreams. Love completes your life. Without love, your life isn't complete, and, therefore, this makes it difficult to achieve true happiness. As the Beatles said, "All you need is love."

From the time we're born, we all have a need for love. And this need remains throughout our entire life. Love definitely feels good. It can give you that warm and fuzzy feeling. Having a lot of love in your life can be a very effective way of reducing your stress levels. Love can keep you healthy mentally, physically, socially, emotionally, and spiritually. Love can improve your overall level of health and happiness.

Here are some of the benefits of love:

Love can be a very effective way of reducing stress levels. When people are in intimate relationships, our adrenaline glands produce dehydroepiandrosterone (DHEA) hormones that act as stress busters and zappers. In addition, the support of someone who loves you can help you cope better when you are facing a stressor.

Love promotes your mental health. The calming effect of DHEA over the mind and body raises the growth of nerves. It is also helpful in restoring the growth of nerves, which results in improved memory and recall. Love makes you feel more relaxed and may put your mind at ease. Furthermore, it makes you feel comforted, warm and fuzzy, connected, important, and cared for.

LOVE, LOVE, LOVE

Love helps you establish an identity and a sense of purpose. Love is great for your mental health.

Love may have an anti-cancer effect. Studies have shown that married people have lower cancer rates than singles. A research conducted at the University of Iowa found that ovarian-cancer patients who had a strong and satisfying relationship with their partners develop more white blood cells, which are desirable for killing cancerous cells. Furthermore, love can give you amazing strength and the will to live, especially when you need it most. This strength may allow you to fight health battles more effectively.

Love can reduce pain. (It can also increase it [lol!]) Love results in more activation in the part of the brain that keeps pain under control. A study has confirmed that married people are less likely to complain of headaches and back pain. The happier the marriage, the greater the effect. Remember: A happy wife is a happy life. A reduced stress level also leads to pain relief, especially if you suffer from things such as chronic headaches. Next time a loved one is in pain, give them a great, big, tight, long hug.

Love gets your blood pumping. It helps provide you with better blood circulation. When you're talking to someone you find attractive, your brain sends impulses to the heart, making it pound faster than normal. This results in increased blood supply to the body, improved circulation and efficient working of all organs. Love gets your blood flowing.

Love can help you live longer. Social isolation, caused by lack of love, increases the risk of early death by up to five times. A study confirmed that married people live longer because they feel loved and connected as opposed to people who are isolated. Furthermore, married people are out-living unmarried people. Another study found that married people have shorter hospital stays and fewer doctor's visits. Researchers believe that this is due to the fact that people in good relationships take better care of themselves. Also, marriage contributes to a decline in drug abuse and heavy drinking, especially among young adults. Love can give us a zest for life. It may give us energy, enthusiasm, and excitement. Love creates a reason to live longer.

CHOOSING TRUE HAPPINESS

Love lowers blood pressure (and sometimes raises it [lol!]). A study has found that happily married people have better blood pressure as compared to singles or unhappily married people. However, singles with a strong social network also did well in the study. Love can relax us and have a soothing, calming effect on our minds and bodies.

Love can provide a reduced risk of heart disease. Expressing your feelings of affection can reduce cholesterol levels. People who express their feelings of affection for loved ones may have significantly lower cholesterol levels than those who don't. Lower cholesterol levels result in reduced chances of a heart attack and other cardiovascular diseases. In addition, expressing yourself in a healthy manner is beneficial to your overall health. Not expressing yourself can be unhealthy and lead to problems. So, express yourself affectionately. For me, holding in my feelings and not expressing myself and having to deal and cope with my father's life were the main causes of my depression.

Love can help you look and feel younger. DHEA acts as an "anti-aging" hormone, which produces feelings of youth and vitality. Adding to that, the increase blood flow to the skin due to the endorphins produced by the body when a person is in love helps keep it soft and smooth, and reduces the development of wrinkles.

Love is much more than just genes, chemicals, and hormones. So, if you are a person who is conscious about health and wellness, learn to love deeply and sincerely. If you want to live longer and happier, then learn to love harder. (2)

You don't need to be married to have love in your life. For those of you who aren't in a committed relationship, make sure to have a strong social network. Single people can be as happy as married people. Perhaps, even happier.

If you choose to spend a lot of time by yourself, then strongly consider getting a dog. A dog is the only creature on Mother Earth that will love you more than you love yourself. The unconditional love that you receive from a dog is priceless. Adopt—don't shop—and perhaps it will be one of the best things that you have ever done in your life. October is National Adopt a Shelter Dog Month.

LOVE, LOVE, LOVE

Dogs are truly amazing companions. We have a mini-goldendoodle named Teddy, and I can't picture my life without him. He's become a big part of my life, and I treasure our time together. Teddy is like a son to me. He brings lots of unconditional love and happiness into our lives. Teddy is constantly giving lots and lots and lots of love to us or receiving lots and lots and lots of love from us. As a result, our home is filled with a lot of love. Humans can learn many lessons from dogs: Live in the present moment, acceptance, unconditional love, loyalty, determination, courage, persistence, kindness, forgiveness (not holding grudges), and how to have fun. Dogs are great role models for humans. It's definitely not a coincidence that GOD spelled backwards is DOG.

One beautiful quality that separates us from other living things is the ability to love. Love is extremely powerful. We have the power to access that emotion whenever we want to display it. We as humans are all connected in some ways: We all have feelings. We all bleed red. And, yes, humans are complex and complicated, but we can choose to be simple and plain. We all have many similarities, however, our differences is what makes us special and unique. Our differences should be appreciated and celebrated. They should bring us together and unite us, not divide us. Diversity is understanding and accepting that each individual is special and unique. And that in itself is a beautiful thing.

Why can't we all do the right thing and love one another? Love is free and available at any time. Let's choose to love one another. Give lots of love and receive lots of love. Choose love and compassion, not anger and hate—it's much better for you and everyone else.

In what ways are you going to love yourself?

How will you start showing a lot of love? How are you going to let love be a bigger part of your life? The world needs more people who love themselves and others. Spread the love—humanity really needs it!

> "I still believe that love is all you need.
> I don't know a better message than that."
> —PAUL MCCARTNEY (3)

CHOOSING TRUE HAPPINESS

"Granny Sheeran told me, when I'm looking for a partner, to fall in love with their eyes because eyes are the only things that don't age. So if you fall in love with their eyes, you'll be in love forever."
—Ed Sheeran (4)

"One word frees us of all the weight and pain of life: That word is *love*."
—Sophocles (5)

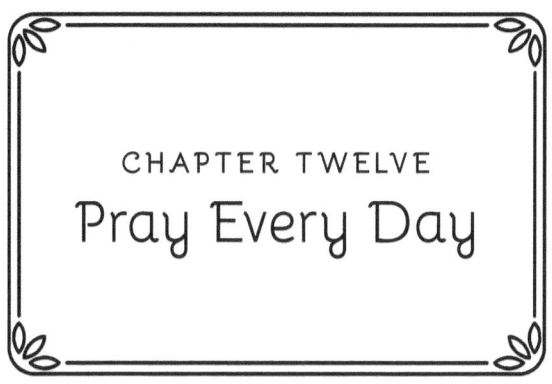

CHAPTER TWELVE
Pray Every Day

"He who has learned to pray has learned the greatest secret
of a holy and happy life."
—WILLIAM LAW (1)

Prayer is defined as the act of praying to God—a solemn request for help or expression of thanks addressed to God.[12]

Prayer is extremely powerful. Perhaps these expressions sound familiar: "Prayer can move mountains" and "A family that prays together, stays together." Prayer gives us hope, help, strength, courage, direction, patience, knowledge, and the opportunity to heal. It's very important to believe in your prayers and trust God to answer them. Believe in God, trust God, have faith in God, thank God, and love God, and your prayers will be answered. God answers prayers according to whatever time he thinks is best.

Prayer builds our relationship with God, connects us directly to God and increases our faith in God. Prayer is one of the most powerful forces in the

---

12 (www.awakenthegreatnesswithin.com)

universe. Think about how beautiful it is that you can directly communicate with the creator of the entire universe. Tell God your needs, and thank him for everything in your life. The most important part of our existence and being is to grow spiritually and love God with all our mind, heart, and soul. Nothing is more important. God always comes first. Your relationship with God is the most important relationship you will ever have here on this Earth. God is omnipotent, omnipresent, and omniscient. God has limitless power, is everywhere, and knows everything.

This is the way it works. The more we pray to God and see him answer those prayers, the more faith we have in him. Therefore, prayer builds faith. However, be patient—it takes time to see that God can do anything. Just because God doesn't answer your prayers doesn't mean he's not listening—he's always listening. He's just got something better in store for you.

Any quality relationship involves communication. Prayer is communicating with God. When we draw close to God, in any way we can, we find a greater happiness and joy in our life. Prayer is about connecting with God. Prayer is our connection with God. Use the *3 Ts: Talk* to God, *thank* God, and *trust* God—you will grow spiritually. Put God first and foremost in your life. The most important relationship you have in your life is your relationship with God. Find your *God Zone*. Get in your *God Zone*. And stay in your *God Zone*.

Prayer reduces worry and enhances contemplation. Choose to pray when worries come your way. Pray more, worry less! Prayer allows us to be forgiven for our mistakes. Learn from our mistakes, and don't keep making the same ones over and over. Prayer gives us the chance to humbly admit our needs and our dependence upon God. In doing so, we reduce our ego, which can really wreak havoc on a person's life. With God, all things are possible, and, without God, nothing is possible.

Prayer empowers us, gives us direction, and brings focus to our lives. Prayer allows us to grow in God's love. Prayer gives us the opportunity to be a better person and do good deeds. Prayer can help us heal and bring peace and love to our lives. Prayer can rejuvenate and energize us. Prayer can allow us to reflect and listen to ourselves. Prayer is therapy. Prayer can get us

PRAY EVERY DAY

through hard times and help us overcome challenging circumstances. When life brings you to your knees, you're in a perfect position to pray. Prayer can allow us to accept difficult people and situations. Set aside time every day to pray. Prayer can work wonders and perform miracles. People who pray on a daily basis are healthier and happier compared to those who do not pray on a daily basis.

God wants us to pray every day. That way, he can be part of our lives. Prayer is a way of expressing our needs and wants. God knows that, if we just ask him, he can help us. Ask, and you shall receive. Always remember that God loves you and really, really wants to have a relationship with you.

Prayer helps us to work out our problems. God can handle whatever you are going through in your life. Bring everything to him in prayer. Whether it's depression, anxiety, anger, frustration, addiction, or grief, God's got you. You should also pray to God if you're feeling confused and have questions. Prayer can reduce confusion and help us to understand. If we turn to God when we don't understand, he will help us to understand why things have happened.

God wants us to think before we speak or act. He wants to make sure we make good choices. God wants us to choose the right road, not a road of temptation. Prayer will give us future guidance from God and show us the correct path. Prayer allows us to talk to God and be with God on an intimate level. Talking with God makes our bond with him stronger, and this will assist us through the trials and tribulations of life. Prayer gives us knowledge and understanding, and allows us to grow in every facet of our lives.

Prayer has many, many benefits. You must pray in order to reap these benefits. Can you think of a better way to build your relationship with God? Pray on a daily basis, and it will have an enormous impact on your life. Prayer will bring more happiness and joy into your life.

> "God speaks in the silence of the heart.
> Listening is the beginning of prayer."
> —Mother Teresa (2)

CHOOSING TRUE HAPPINESS

"Love to pray. Feel often during the day the need for prayer, and take trouble to pray. Prayer enlarges the heart until it is capable of containing God's gift of Himself. Ask and seek, and your heart will grow big enough to receive Him and keep Him as your own.'
—MOTHER TERESA (3)

"Always pray to have eyes that see the best in people, a heart that forgives the worst, a mind that forgets the bad, and a soul that never loses faith in God."
—ANONYMOUS (4)

CHAPTER THIRTEEN
Sleep Well and Rejuvenate

"True silence is the rest of the mind; it is to the spirit what sleep is to the body, nourishment and refreshment."
—WILLIAM PENN (1)

There's nothing like a great night's sleep. Sleep is an active state that affects both your physical and mental well-being. A deep sleep can leave you feeling refreshed, renewed, and rejuvenated in the morning. Great sleep can give you a whole new outlook, which can be crucial when you are going through a challenging time. What a difference a day can make when you get a good night's sleep. Considering how hectic life can be, it's very important to get a great night's sleep. This can help you hit the reset button, which can be a beautiful thing. Sleep is my pleasure and retreat.

A great night's sleep helps our body rest and replenishes its energy levels. In addition, a great night's sleep can be an effective way to help you solve issues, relax your mind, cope with stress and stressful events, and recover from being ill. Other benefits may include being more productive, emotionally balanced, and in a better mood. Further benefits may include your body repairing and regenerating tissue, building bone and muscle, and strengthening your immune system.

What happens if we don't get enough sleep? Too little sleep can cause:

* More pain
* Confusion and inability to think clearly and function properly
* Irritability
* Fatigue
* Nervousness and anxiety
* Weaker immune system
* Depression
* Memory loss

Furthermore, chronic long-term insufficient sleep can increase your chance of developing cardiovascular disease, weight gain, and diabetes.

You might be thinking to yourself: *How much sleep do I need?* The amount of sleep a person needs varies, depending on their age and other various factors. An infant needs about 16 to 18 hours of sleep daily. On average, teenagers need about 9 hours of sleep per day (although I know some parents wish their teenage children would sleep more than that [lol!]). Most adults require about 7-9 hours of sleep daily. Please understand that your body and mind *will not adapt* to getting less sleep than needed. Also, the amount of sleep you need increases if you are behind on your sleep. Therefore, don't fall behind on your sleep, otherwise, you'll have to play catch-up.

So how do we get a good night's sleep?

* Pray
* Talk to your doctor about increasing your tryptophan levels
* Have some chamomile tea before bed
* Talk to your doctor about melatonin
* Take a warm bath (but not right before bed)
* Have a glass of wine around 6 p.m.

SLEEP WELL AND REJUVENATE

- Read
- Talk to your doctor about lavender essential oil
- Drink warm milk
- Master meditation and slow, deep, focused breathing
- Keep your room dark
- Use these *I* statements: *I am calm. I am relaxed.* Say these *I* statements out loud after taking a slow, deep, focused breath. Your mind believes what you tell it.
- Talk to your doctor about valerian root
- Relaxing music
- Put a pillow between your legs (make sure it is comfortable and the correct size)
- Maintain a *regular* sleep schedule (go to sleep and wake up at about the same time every day)
- Exercise (leave at least 3 to 4 hours before you go to sleep)
- Earplugs and/or eye mask
- Avoid caffeine and nicotine
- Hug somebody for at least 20 seconds

Sound sleep is a necessity in order for infants to develop and grow properly. Great sleep is also crucial for the development and well-being of children, teenagers, and adults. Sound sleep can work wonders. Do everything in your power to help yourself get a great night's sleep. It will be well worth your effort. You must get sound sleep in order to have a happy life. When was the last time you had a great night's sleep? Sweet dreams!

> "I love to sleep. I'd sleep all day if I could."
> —MILEY CYRUS (2)

> "Sleep is the golden chain that ties health and our bodies together."
> —THOMAS DEKKER (3)

CHOOSING TRUE HAPPINESS

"The best bridge between despair and hope is a good night's sleep."
—E. Joseph Cossman (4)

CHAPTER FOURTEEN
Hugs Feel Great

"When we hug, our hearts connect, and we know that we are not separate beings. Hugging with mindfulness and concentration can bring reconciliation, healing, understanding, and much happiness."

—NHAT HANH (1)

When it comes to hugging, we usually use our hugs to express our love for our family and friends. Hugs are a way of communicating and providing comfort.

Most of us know hugging as a way to express affection. Also, hugs can be used for saying hello or goodbye, especially if we are happy to see someone or sad to see someone leave. However, have you ever thought about the benefits of hugging for its own sake? Believe it or not, there's actually a science behind hugs. The truth may surprise you: Hugs boost our happiness levels—and there's scientific research to prove this.

CHOOSING TRUE HAPPINESS

Oxytocin is known as the love drug. It calms your nervous system and boosts positive emotions. A good hug is a quick way to get oxytocin flowing in your body. The flow of oxytocin in our bodies results in great health benefits:

* It plays a powerful role in protecting the heart
* It reduces free-radical formation and other inflammatory markers, decreasing the risk for a heart attack
* It can increase your social connections and a sense of belonging
* It lowers your blood pressure, which is especially helpful if you are feeling anxious
* It lowers your cortisol, the stress hormone, enabling a higher quality of sleep
* It releases endorphins and serotonin into the blood vessels, which cause pleasure and negate pain and sadness
* It balances out the nervous system
* It strengthens the immune system
* It helps to stretch the facial muscles, erase age lines, and slow the aging process
* It decreases the chances of developing heart problems
* It helps fight excess weight and prolongs life
* It relaxes muscles, releases tension in the body, and takes away pain
* Hugging for an extended time lifts one's serotonin levels, elevating mood and creating happiness

The nurturing touch of hugging may make us healthier, more relaxed, age slower, live longer, and help us fight depression. A proper, deep hug, where the hearts are pressing together not only improves both psychological and physical development but also helps to build a good immune system, decrease the risk of heart disease, and decrease levels of the stress hormone cortisol in women. Hugging can stimulate and sharpen the senses, contribute to our sense of connectedness, cause us to feel calm and happier, and protect us against the effects of loneliness, isolation, and anger.

HUGS FEEL GREAT

Who would've thought that hugging had such amazing benefits? Some reports have even shown hugs can reduce pain. Also, studies have shown that couples who hug more are more likely to stay together. Hugs are a beautiful thing. Hugging teaches us how to give and receive. Hugging can also teach us to let go and be present in the moment. And what better way to live than in the present moment? Living in the present moment as much as possible is absolutely the best way to live. Hugging encourages empathy and understanding. Hugging also builds trust and a sense of safety, helps with open and honest communication, and boosts self-esteem. Furthermore, hugging allows us to connect with our heart and feelings. Hugging is like a handshake of the hearts. Hugging therapy is definitely a powerful way of healing. (2)

Now here's the important part. It must be a very good hug—meaning it has to last at least 20 seconds. I think we can all spare 20 seconds out of our day to give someone a really good hug. Do you think you give enough hugs in a day? Probably not! So, spring into action, and start hugging. I love hugging. When I give hugs, I make it a point not to be the first one to let go. When *you* hug, don't be the first to let go. Hugs are free, convenient, and beneficial to our overall well-being.

So, what are you waiting for? Hugs can make you happier, healthier, more relaxed; they can even improve our relationships. Hugs are powerful. So, start spreading the happiness by hugging. Take this hug challenge: Hug somebody every day for at least 20 seconds. The world can definitely use more hugging. If I could, I would give everybody in the world a hug.

> "A hug is a wonderful thing. It's a marvelous gift to share. It's a grand way to say, 'I care.' A hug communicates support, security, affection, unity, and belonging. A hug shows compassion. A hug brings delight. A hug charms the senses. A hug touches the soul."
> —Bob Stoess (3)

CHOOSING TRUE HAPPINESS

"Hugs are one of the reasons God gave us arms. So, stretch out your arms to someone today. Reach out to those you love. It will warm the heart of the giver and give light to the soul of the recipient."
—Bob Stoess (4)

"Be a love pharmacist: dispense hugs like medicine—they are!"
—Terri Guillemets (5)

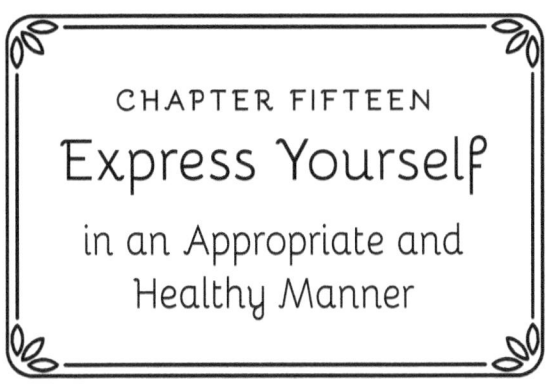

CHAPTER FIFTEEN
Express Yourself
in an Appropriate and Healthy Manner

"Be crazy. Be stupid. Be silly. Be weird. Be whatever. Because life is too short to be anything but happy."
—Hoda Kotb (1)

If everybody were the same, the world would be a boring place. It's important that we see ourselves for who we are and that we celebrate and honor what makes us special and unique. Life can be much better once you value and appreciate yourself for simply being you. In a world where conformity is the norm, it can be difficult to truly *be yourself*. It's easy to give in to peer pressure and try to be like the majority. But you don't have to be like everyone else. You have a choice to be whoever you want to be.[13]

---

13 *60 Be Yourself Quotes and Sayings to Inspire Your Best Life*, Norbert Juma, Lead Editor September 25, 2020 6:00 a.m. EST https://everydaypower.com/be-yourself-quotessayings/

CHOOSING TRUE HAPPINESS

Expressing yourself in an appropriate manner is very important in maintaining a happy and healthy life. Expressing yourself can help us keep in touch and deal with our emotions in a positive manner. There are many methods you can use in order to express yourself effectively and appropriately. These methods include:

* Prayer
* Laugh, laugh, and laugh some more (use your sense of humor as much as possible)
* Sing
* Dance
* Cry (Crying is a sign of strength and humanness)
* Use a daily journal to write in
* Exercise
* Talk therapy
* Art (draw, color, paint, sketch)
* Listen to music or play a musical instrument
* Tatoos
* Talk to a friend, family member, or anybody you trust
* Hairstyle
* Clothing style

Prayer is a phenomenal and powerful way to express yourself in a positive manner. Praying every day can help you manage and express your thoughts and emotions, share your concerns and needs, and give thanks for all the blessings in your life. I pray every day, once in the morning and once at night.

Laughter is a great and healthy way to express yourself. Learn to laugh at yourself, and don't be so serious. Find the humor in things and situations. And make it a point to laugh every day. Don't take life too seriously. I make it a point to try and laugh every day. I find the humor in many things.

There's nothing wrong with singing in the shower or dancing when you come out. Give it a try, and belt out your favorite song next time you take a

EXPRESS YOURSELF IN AN APPROPRIATE AND HEALTHY...

shower. If that's not for you, then, when you come home, put some music on, and sing and/or dance. Make it fun, and enjoy yourself.

Crying is a sign of strength and humanness. We need to learn to express our emotions and that it's okay to cry. Real men cry! Crying is a natural, healthy, human response to a range of emotions, including frustration, anger, sadness, grief, and embarrassment. There's nothing like a good cry to let it all out. Unfortunately, our society views crying as a flaw or sign of weakness. In fact, crying is a coping strategy and self-soothing behavior. It may help you deal with stress, improve your mood, and restore emotional balance. Crying can help to regulate your emotions, calm yourself down, and reduce your own distress. It can help relieve frustration, anger, sadness, grief, and embarrassment. Our society needs to understand and convey, once and for all, that crying is not a flaw or sign of weakness. We are all emotional beings, and we all have the right to cry whenever and wherever we want. We were all given the ability to cry for a reason. We all need to cry at one point in our life. Do you sometimes want to cry, but just can't seem to shed a single tear? Don't hold back your tears! There is freedom in every drop.

Writing in a journal on a daily basis may have numerous benefits. If *daily* journal entries aren't your cup of tea, then write in a journal *as needed*. Writing is a great way to express yourself. It may be a lot easier for someone to write about their feelings than to talk about them. You may even learn a great deal about yourself from your journaling. You may start to see patterns regarding your feelings and actions, or journaling might assist you in getting to the root of some issues. A journal might provide you with the answers that you've been looking for, including causes and solutions. It's up to you whether you want to share your journal with others or keep it confidential. Perhaps you may choose to share things and keep other things private. Do whatever you are comfortable with. Writing, at certain times in my life, has been therapeutic for me.

Exercising is one of the best outlets you can incorporate into your life. It's great for your health and phenomenal for stress. Exercising at least 3 to 4 times a week will have a positive impact on your life and your overall happiness level. And it doesn't have to be boring. Pick activities that you may enjoy such as basketball, tennis, jump rope, walking, running, spin classes, bike riding, Zumba, or kick boxing. Your body will release feel-good chemicals, and your stress level will go down. You may even feel better about yourself and improve your self-image, self-esteem and self-concept. I make sure I exercise 3 times a week.

Talk therapy is an effective way to communicate your thoughts and feelings. Talk therapy can help you work out issues and find positive solutions. Whether you are stressed out or suffer from a mental-health problem, talk therapy can definitely help. Talking about your thoughts and feelings is good for you. It may help you deal with overwhelming issues and help you through the challenging and struggling times. Talk therapy can help you find out what is really bothering you and explore options for a solution. There's absolutely no reason to feel embarrassed or ashamed to go to a therapist. You should feel very proud of yourself if you make the decision to go see a talk therapist. We all need someone to talk to at some point in our lives, especially during challenging times.

Sometimes a family member or friend isn't enough, and you need to seek out a trained and experienced professional talk therapist. Find somebody you are comfortable with, and trust the person you choose. Understand the different types of talk therapy, and find the right person for you. Cognitive Behavioral Therapy (CBT) is a treatment that can work wonders for you. You will be on your way to improving your life. Have confidence in the trained professional you choose. Believe that the person you pick will help you. Personally, I have gone to see a professional talk therapist, and it has worked extremely well. I continue to use the information I learned in sessions every day. Reaching out for help for yourself or others is a sign of honesty, intelligence, strength, and courage; it's a great and responsible choice.

Many people use art to express themselves. Drawing, painting, coloring, sketching, and sculpting can be very therapeutic. Some may choose to use these methods to express how they feel, relieve stress, enhance their creativity,

EXPRESS YOURSELF IN AN APPROPRIATE AND HEALTHY...

and improve their social skills. Art can help you take your mind off troubling thoughts and help redirect and refocus you.

Sometimes people can't say what they want to say. Perhaps they're at a loss for words or just don't want to talk about it. This is when art can be very beneficial. Let the piece of work or project do the talking for you. Art may give you the opportunity to transform negative emotions into something positive. It can help you to relax, focus, develop patience, and improve problem-solving skills. If art is not your thing, perhaps you can take a trip to a museum. Make it a memorable experience. Maybe you can write or talk about the exhibits you enjoyed the most and how those pieces of art made you feel. Art can be a very positive and powerful part of your life. Art can be a productive channel that you can utilize throughout your entire life.

Having music in your life is a fantastic way to improve your happiness level. Listening to music can be extremely therapeutic and help people deal with and express their emotions. It's very important to be in control of your emotions throughout your life. Emotions can make us erratic and vulnerable, allowing us to easily lose control and make poor decisions.

Music is an amazing way to work through the dark sides of our emotions. In some countries, music has even been used for recovery therapy for addictions and illnesses. I listen to music every single day. I can't picture my life without it.

Have you ever listened to a song that nailed exactly what you were going through and how you were feeling? I can tell you from personal experience that I have listened to those songs that hit home. After my parents' divorce, when I was around 15, I was devastated. There was this one song that I would listen to over and over again. The song was "The Heart of the Matter" by Don Henley. This song definitely comforted me in the beginning of my parents' divorce and helped me cope a little bit.

The Chinese philosopher Confucius said long ago, "Music produces a kind of pleasure which human nature cannot do without." Playing a musical instrument has many benefits and can bring joy to you and to everyone around you.

CHOOSING TRUE HAPPINESS

> Playing a musical instrument fosters your self-expression and relieves stress. It's your instrument, so you can play whatever you want on it! The more advanced you become on an instrument, the greater you'll be able to play what you want and how you want. Music is an art—just like an artist can paint his/her emotions onto a canvas, so can a musician play a piece with emotion. This has proven to relieve stress and can be a great form of therapy. In fact, music therapy has been useful in treating children and teens with autism, depression, and other disorders. Music is usually expressing something and sending a message. We need to be attentive and pay attention to the message. Music helps keep us quiet, develops our listening and memory skills, and keeps us company when we are alone. Furthermore, it can create a sense of achievement and promote your social skills. Music can be uplifting, soothing, and relaxing.[14]

Music is therapeutic. It enhances the quality of your life, provides companionship and a friend. It is a form of expression, inspiration, entertainment; it's a valuable resource, and it's fun. The power and benefits of music are extraordinary.

---

[14] Lwcmusic.org *18 Benefits of Playing a Musical Instrument* by Michael Matthews © EffectiveMusicTeaching.com

EXPRESS YOURSELF IN AN APPROPRIATE AND HEALTHY...

What would the world be like without music? Music should be a big part of everybody's life. You should ask yourself, "What role does music play in my life?" Music is a fantastic way to improve your happiness level.

Once again, talking is great for us. Another healthy way to express ourselves is to talk to a friend, family member, or somebody we trust. Personally, my friends and family have helped me face the storms of life. They have definitely helped me endure and get through life's storms. I strongly believe there are hidden blessings in the storms of life. We need to find the silver lining in the cloud. We might not see it at the time, however, it might be what's best for what's yet to come. Also, be realistic and remember that we *all* hit rough patches at one point or another in our lives. Be sure to utilize your positive support system and see things using a positive lens. It could make all the difference in getting through a challenging time. Regardless of your circumstances, choose to sing, dance, and laugh right now.

Other ways to express ourselves include, but are not limited to, the way we dress, our hairstyle, and tattoos. All these ways of self-expression can say a lot about someone and be healthy, depending on how a person utilizes them in their life. Personally, I have a tattoo on each arm. My right arm has my daughter's name—"Isabella"—and her date of birth in cursive writing and her footprints from when she was born. My left arm has the same tattoo, except that it's dedicated to my other daughter, Olivia, who was born on my birthday. Tattoos can be beautiful pieces of art, depending, of course, on the type of tattoo a person gets.

What could happen if we don't express ourselves in a healthy manner? We could turn to other outlets that can be destructive and unhealthy. Years ago, I was never a person to talk about my feelings. I would hold everything in and let it build up. Repressing your feelings is extremely unhealthy and can be detrimental and dangerous for your physical and mental health. Instead of talking about what was upsetting me and dealing with it, I chose to ignore it, hold it in, and shut down. Not dealing directly with my feelings and issues caused me to sleep a lot and deprived me of motivation. All my frustration and anger was bottled up inside me. I got clinically depressed and went through many ups and downs through the years. I suffered from depression starting around 15 to around my early twenties.

Please learn from my mistake. The moral of the story is to deal head-on with managing your thoughts and emotions and do not repress/hold in your feelings. Talk about or express what is bothering you, and don't hold it in. Deal with your issues directly, and face them with determination. Grab the bull by the horns and immediately deal with any problem or concern that is affecting your thoughts, emotions, and actions. And, when necessary, get to the root of your issue. Turning your anger and any other negative emotion inward is a recipe for disaster. Do not hold in your feelings. Express and rejoice or repress and suffer.

Express your anger and other negative emotions immediately and appropriately. You don't want your negative emotions to be repeated over and over, constantly recreating painful experiences. Stop the cycle; don't identify with the negative emotion, and be in the present moment. Be, just be. We should face our negative emotions and then let go of them the moment they arise. Repressing and not accepting our negative emotions will provide us with unhappiness. Sooner or later, you will have to deal with your negative emotions, better sooner than later. Ideally, deal appropriately with the negative emotion as soon as it happens. Now is much better than later when dealing with negative emotions.

Unhealthy outlets that people turn to, consciously or unconsciously, include smoking, drugs, alcohol, gambling, undereating or overeating, shopping compulsively, too much or too little sleep, and any other compulsions or addictions. These unhealthy, alternate methods of coping will not make the problem go away. In fact, these methods might compound the problem and make it worse. These methods might numb us, relieve stress at the moment, provide an escape, and help us forget about what is upsetting us momentarily. Guess what? When we wake up the next day, the problem will still be there and may even be bigger.

It is not a wise decision to use these self-destructive behaviors as coping mechanisms. Instead choose to use positive coping skills when going through

EXPRESS YOURSELF IN AN APPROPRIATE AND HEALTHY...

challenging times. All of us hit a point in our lives where we can self-destruct or help ourselves, make good choices, and make the necessary changes. Make it a point to lift yourself up and move forward. The choice is yours. Our lives are shaped by the choices that we make.

Expressing yourself in a healthy manner is crucial in order to have a happy life. Take a moment, and reflect on how you express yourself in your life. Ask yourself if the methods you choose are healthy or unhealthy. Honest or dishonest? Effective or ineffective? Helpful or hurtful? Reflecting on your choices of how you express yourself can provide valuable insight for living a happy life. Step outside your comfort zone, so that you may begin to express yourself, change, grow, learn, and live.

God made us all different for a reason. Nevertheless, we are all one, all God's Children. If everybody were the same, the world would be a boring place.

> "Live life as though nobody is watching, and express yourself as though everyone is listening."
> —Nelson Mandela (2)

> "You've got to express yourself in life, and it is better out than in. What you reveal, you heal."
> —Chris Martin (3)

> "Don't keep all your feelings sheltered—express them. Don't ever let life shut you up."
> —Dr. Steve Maraboli (4)

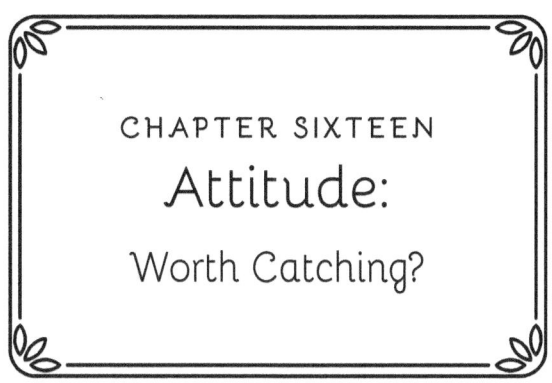

CHAPTER SIXTEEN

Attitude:
Worth Catching?

"You cannot control what happens to you, but you can control your attitude toward what happens to you, and in that, you will be mastering change rather than allowing it to master you."

—BRIAN TRACY (1)

I will define attitude as *"a settled way of thinking* or feeling about someone or something, typically one that is reflected in a person's behavior."[15]

Attitude and belief are the thermostats that regulate what we accomplish in life. Our attitude is directly connected to our accomplishments. A positive attitude will allow a person to get more done and live a happier life. Attitude is just as important, if not more important, than ability. A positive mental attitude is a game changer.

A person's attitude affects every aspect of their life. Our relationships, our level of appreciation, our perspective, and, most importantly, our view about

---

15 (www.encyclopedia.com)

CHOOSING TRUE HAPPINESS

God, among other things, are greatly affected by our attitude. Remember these three very important components for true happiness—**R**elationships, **A**ppreciation, and **P**erspective (RAP).

It's imperative to have the right attitude in order to live a truly happy life. Happiness is an attitude. Also, the choices we make in our life are affected by our attitude. The choices we make mean everything. Our lives are shaped by the choices that we make. We *choose* to be happy or sad *despite* our surroundings and circumstances. The greater part of our happiness or unhappiness depends upon our disposition, how we view our surroundings and circumstances, and how we think and feel about them—not the surroundings and circumstances themselves. Our surroundings and circumstances don't define who we are; we define who we are. Being happy means to look at things a certain way and have a certain attitude. We can't control everything that happens to us, but we can control our attitude toward what happens to us. And if we maintain a positive attitude toward life events, then we will conquer change and greatly increase our chances to live a happy life.

Our thinking shapes our attitudes. Our thinking is everything. The inner dialogue we live with every day is what creates our attitudes. *Attitude talk* is a way to override your past negative programming by erasing or replacing it with a conscious, positive internal voice that helps you face new directions. Your internal conversation—that little voice you listen to all day long—acts like a seed in that it programs your brain and affects your behavior. Take a closer look at your inner dialogue and what you are saying to yourself and, more importantly, if you are listening to and believing that inner voice. Attitude and self-talk are directly connected to one another. (2)

Thoughts come and go like the clouds. Thoughts are not facts. Thoughts are not real, except that we are aware of them. Thoughts are not reality. Automated Negative Thoughts (ANTS) need to be ignored. Pay attention to the positive thoughts.

Our attitudes shape our emotions. Our thinking is directly connected to our emotions. How we think affects how we feel. Therefore, positive thinking may generate positive emotions. Negative thinking may generate negative

ATTITUDE: WORTH CATCHING?

emotions. It all starts with our thinking. Furthermore, positive thinking may trigger positive events. Negative thinking may trigger negative events. Train and discipline your mind to focus on the positive. Your mind will become dark if you focus on people or situations that displease you.

Our attitude affects our health. Our health is our greatest wealth. Studies have shown that people with a positive attitude toward life tend to get sick less often than those with a negative attitude. Even though this concept may be difficult to believe, these studies in the mind-body connection are showing us that our minds play a major role in influencing our level of wellness. The mind-body concept is defined as the interaction that takes place between our thoughts, our body, and our external world.

A new science that studies this link is called psychoneuroimmunology (PNI). PNI describes ways in which our emotions and attitude, both positive and negative, can affect our health and also the outcome of medical treatment.

How do we help someone who has a poor attitude? Ah, yes—an attitude adjustment. Attitudes are contagious. Surround yourself with positive people and positive energy. Poor attitudes are counterproductive for achieving true happiness in your life. Ask yourself this question, "Is my attitude worth catching?" Answer the question honestly. If the answer is "No," then you need to make some changes. Your attitude is a crucial component in your happiness. Ask yourself, "Is my attitude worth catching, or do I need to adjust my attitude?" You need to have the right attitude in order to achieve true happiness in your life.

Ready to start? Here are 10 ways to create a positive attitude:

1. **Create awareness.**
   Put a rubber band on your wrist as a reminder to notice your thoughts. When you look at the rubber band, take note of your thoughts and feelings. Sometimes you can catch yourself in

the middle of a rumination or worry. Other times, you might notice you feel anxious, irritated, or sad, but you aren't immediately sure why. When this happens, ask yourself what the thoughts are that have produced these feelings. By paying attention this way, you'll see how often you get caught up in negative thinking.

2. **Break the spell.**
   After you've spent two or three days noticing your thoughts and feelings, it's time to do something about them. Keep the rubber band on your wrist, and every time you notice negative thinking, gently pop the rubber band, or move it to the other wrist. You want a physical pattern-interrupt to break up the mental looping of negative thoughts. Then mentally identify and label what you were doing. "Oh, there's that negative thinking again. There are those thoughts and feelings popping up again." I say to myself, "There goes those brain farts again." Then I usually start laughing. You want to dis-identify with the thoughts—they are separate from *you as a person*. It's important to recognize your thoughts as random products of consciousness instead of seeing them as reality. Just be an observer of your thoughts. You are not your thoughts.

ATTITUDE: WORTH CATCHING?

3. **Fill in the blank.**
   Once you interrupt the negative thought and identify it, you need to switch gears entirely. You can't leave a mental void, or you'll go directly back to negative thinking, which is an entrenched habit that's become natural for your brain. You must retrain your brain to think differently. So, after you pop the rubber band, redirect your thoughts or actions. One way to do this is by reframing your thought to disprove it or make it positive. For example, if you're thinking, "I'll never get this project finished on time," then say to yourself, "No, that's not true. I can and will get it done on time. I always have in the past, and I will again." Even if you don't believe this totally, say it out loud or to yourself. Acknowledge any solid evidence you have that counters your negative thought.
   Be rigorous in your efforts at redirecting your thoughts, just as you'd continue to put a toddler back in a time-out chair when they keep getting up. Eventually, your mind will know you mean business. You can also use positive action to replace negative thinking. If you find yourself ruminating over something unpleasant, get up and do something that will occupy your mind and distract you from your thoughts.

CHOOSING TRUE HAPPINESS

4. **Practice daily gratitude.**
   With all of our negative thinking, sometimes it's hard to see how much is truly wonderful about your life. To appreciate how great life really is, you must be intentional about it. I'd suggest keeping a gratitude journal, as writing tends to reinforce thinking. It's good to write in this journal at night, before you go to bed, as you will fill your mind with positivity before you drift into sleep. You may be in the midst of a crisis or worry, but that doesn't negate all of your many, many blessings. Write down each one in your journal, and as you write, really focus on the gratitude item and flood your mind with feelings of gratefulness. Do this every day, even if you're repeating the same items over and over. This will help you keep gratitude at the forefront of your mind rather than in the dark recesses.

5. **Stop reacting.**
   Small negative events during your day can trigger a cascade of pessimistic or angry thoughts and feelings. Someone says something rude to you. You comment back to them. They say something else. You go brood about it for hours. Traffic is bumper-to-bumper, and you're in a hurry. You honk your horn and feel your blood pressure rising. It takes you hours to calm down. Everyday life presents us with a

ATTITUDE: WORTH CATCHING?

multitude of dirty little tricks to goad us into negativity. But as the CEO of your mind, you can choose how you want to react. Sure, you can get pissed off, hurt, or frustrated—but you'll lose hours of your day that could be joyful. Instead, mindfully choose how you want to react. You know difficult things will happen on occasion, so mentally prepare. Teach yourself to take some slow, deep, focused, calming breaths. While we are in the middle of a difficult situation, it often feels as though it is never going to change. That's because your mind is tricking you and lying to you. Don't get tricked and believe the lies. Instead, think to yourself, "This, too, shall pass." And take a slow, deep, focused breath.

Decide on a better way to respond that minimizes negativity. Acknowledge your knee-jerk reactions, but consciously decide not to follow them. If possible, try to find humor in the inanities and frustrations of life, as they are part of the human condition.

6. **Find positive people.**
   We tend to absorb and reflect the emotions and attitudes of those we spend time with. If you're hanging around negative people who complain and worry much of the time, then you are bound to catch their ailment. You may need to make some hard decisions

about who you spend time with, but if someone had a contagious disease, you'd have no trouble creating a boundary between you and them. Negativity is a contagious disease. Find people who uplift you and who are positive, happy, and confident. Do your best to spend less time with people who pull you down.

7. **Have more fun.**
   We get so caught up in the serious business of life that we forget to simply have fun. When was the last time you played a game, rode a bike, flew a kite, or did anything carefree and non-competitive? We need daily fun to balance the stresses and demands of our complicated lives.
   If you can't remember what feels *fun* to you, go back to your childhood and think about fun activities. I have a friend who swings on her children's swing set for relaxation and pleasure. Be vigilant in making fun part of your life.

8. **Turn off the news.**
   Every time I watch the news, I feel worried and sad. A reporter might cover a story on a new health scare, and, of course, I worry about that for myself.
   The never-ending coverage on COVID-19, terrorism, shootings, politics, and natural disasters makes us feel anxious and threatened.

ATTITUDE: WORTH CATCHING?

Yes, there is plenty of bad news, and we need to stay informed. But there's plenty of good news as well. There are plenty of positive, happy, uplifting things going on in the world. So, make a choice to limit the amount of news you watch, and instead find programs, podcasts, blogs, books, and articles that inspire and motivate you. Seek out positive information to fill your mind.

9. **Simplify your life.**
   The busier and more complicated your life is, the more difficult it will be to remain positive. When you have too many demands and obligations, with little time for fun, reflection, relationships, or exercise, the more stressed and unhappy you are bound to feel. We often resort to buying things to soothe our feelings, but all of these material things create stress as well, as you must store them, take care of them, and pay for them.
   Too much stuff drains your psychic energy. Just the act of simplifying—dropping things from your to-do list and getting rid of stuff will make you feel lighter and more positive. Schedule a few days to streamline your life, giving yourself plenty of time and space for your most important life values and activities.

10. **Spend time with friends and family.**
    Quality time spent with the people we love and cherish most is the best way to develop

a positive attitude. People on their deathbeds report that their biggest regret is not spending more time with friends and family.
Be proactive in making time for those you love. Initiate more family events, as well as one-on-one time with your spouse or partner, your children, and your friends. Create rituals and traditions that are meaningful and happy.

Mindfully choose to avoid family drama or conflict, and speak words of love, affirmation, and healing to serve as an example and inspiration to others in your sphere. Mindfully choose to not get involved in arguments or conflict with others. Try this challenge: When you speak to people, speak to them as if it's the last time you will ever speak to them. Words of love, respect, kindness, compassion, and encouragement should flow from your tongue.

Having a positive mental attitude involves making mind shifts and recognizing how much control you have over your thoughts. As you work toward managing and changing your thoughts, and as you choose positive behaviors and actions that are healthy and uplifting, over time, you'll see that positivity is your fallback position. Even during difficult times, you'll have the inner resources to turn yourself around and regain your happy state of mind.[16]

Be honest with yourself, and reflect on your attitude. In order to be happy, you need to have the right attitude. What type of attitude do you have? Is it positive, or do you need to make some changes? Perceive life with a grateful attitude. Attitudes are contagious, is yours worth catching?

> "Everything can be taken from a man but one thing: the last of the human freedoms—to choose one's attitude in any given set of circumstances, to choose one's own way."
> —VIKTOR FRANKL (3)

---

[16] *Positive Mental Attitude: 10 Mindsets for Happiness* [November 2, 2014] by Barrie Davenport, https://liveboldandbloom.com/11/mindfulness/positive-mental-attitude

ATTITUDE: WORTH CATCHING?

"For success, attitude is equally as important as ability."
—Walter Scott (4)

"It is our attitude toward life that determines life's attitude toward us. We get back what we put out."
—Earl Nightingale (5)

CHAPTER SEVENTEEN
Dream On

"Dreams can come true, but there is a secret. They're realized through the magic of persistence, determination, commitment, passion, practice, focus, and hard work. They happen a step at a time, manifested over years, not weeks."[17]
—Elbert Hubbard (1)

I will define dreams as *"a condition or achievement* that is desired and longed for; an aspiration, goal, ambition, a cherished hope."[18]

Think big, dream big, achieve big things. Don't be afraid to follow your dreams. Step outside your comfort zone, and dream. Growth happens when you leave the known and enter the unknown. It's never too late to follow your dreams, and you're never too old to follow your dreams. Don't let fear hold you back. Fear is an illusion—it exists only in our mind. My dream is to help millions of people conquer depression and anxiety. This is one of the main reasons I wrote this book.

---
17 I can definitely relate to this quote. I started this book around 2010.
18 www.thefreedictionary.com

CHOOSING TRUE HAPPINESS

Our dreams give us purpose, direction, and something to strive for. Our dreams challenge us and bring out the best in us. Our dreams can shape who we are. Dreams can give us the courage to grow up and be who we really are meant to be. Believe in your dreams, and find the courage to follow them. Shoot for the stars, and you might just land on the moon. Leave no stone unturned. Find and create your own path. What are you interested in? What are your talents? Focus on your interests and talents. Everybody has interests and talents. I highly recommend reading *5 Steps to Living Your Dreams* by Deepak Chopra, M.D.

Throughout our entire lifetime, through all our experiences, we need to consistently learn and grow as human beings. Make everything in life a learning experience—live and learn (Experiences = Life Lessons). Experience can give you the power, confidence, courage, and knowledge to *be you*. Show growth on a daily basis, and eventually you will see big results. Be consistent, patient, and determined. Remember, you have to start somewhere, but the key is to start. When you continue to dream, you will find it easier to do things that you once found difficult. You will grow, and your comfort zone will expand.

Dreaming means to create a deliberate vision for the future. Dreams can help you take control of your life and keep moving you forward. We must continually move forward in all aspects of our life: spiritually, mentally, socially, emotionally, intellectually, and physically. We have a duty to ourselves to constantly improve. Be accountable to yourself.

The key is to find a greater purpose in life. When you have a greater purpose in life, you'll be more motivated and engaged, and motivation and engagement will give you more results and satisfaction in your life. After all, dreaming is a higher form of engagement.

Do not let your circumstances dictate your dreams. Too many talented people allow themselves to be victims of their circumstances. The difference between those who achieve their dreams and those who don't achieve their dreams is belief, persistence, determination, and effort.

DREAM ON

Always remember that your life is shaped by the choices that you make. And no matter what life brings, we always have the power to choose. You choose the path that you take and the life that you live. No one else chooses the life you live besides you. Whatever you choose to do, do it the best possible way you can do it. Are you currently choosing the life you want to live?

The only way you can get started on the road to achieving your dreams is to be willingly committed. Achieving a dream requires constant, consistent, and committed effort. And staying committed, under any and all circumstances, can be difficult. Know what your dream realistically takes to achieve; don't make it harder than what it really takes to achieve the dream. Actually, your dream can be easier than you think it is to achieve. And you don't have to be amazing in order to start, but you have to start in order to be amazing. Remember, humans are very capable of extraordinary accomplishments.

You need to ask yourself, "What level of commitment would this take on my part?" Compare the level of commitment required to the reward at the end. Great deal? Or not such a great deal? Are you willing to commit to your dreams?

On a daily basis, in all areas of your life, be loving, respectful, kind, compassionate, empathetic, honest, and moral—and show integrity. Have the courage to do the right thing. Support and do what you say. If you talk the talk, then walk the walk. Be a person of your word. I strive to continually be a man of my word.

Figure out what your dreams are, and choose to relentlessly pursue them. Know the level of commitment needed and the requirements for you to accomplish and fulfill that dream. Work on your dream on a daily basis. Before you know it, your dream will become a reality. Do not let a day go by where you don't do something toward fulfilling your dream, even if it's for only 10 to 20 minutes a day. Live for the day; tomorrow isn't promised to anyone. One of my favorite songs is "Dream On," by Aerosmith. For me, the song is about never giving up on your dreams. Whatever happens, dream on! Keep dreaming, people. *Dream on, dream on, dream on!*

CHOOSING TRUE HAPPINESS

"If you can dream it, you can do it.
Your limits are all within yourself."
—Brian Tracy (2)

"To understand the heart and mind of a person, look not at what he has already achieved, but at what he aspires to."
—Khalil Gibran (3)

"How do you go from where you are to where you wanna be? And I think you have to have an enthusiasm for life. You have to have a dream, a goal. And you have to be willing to work for it."
—Jim Valvano (4)

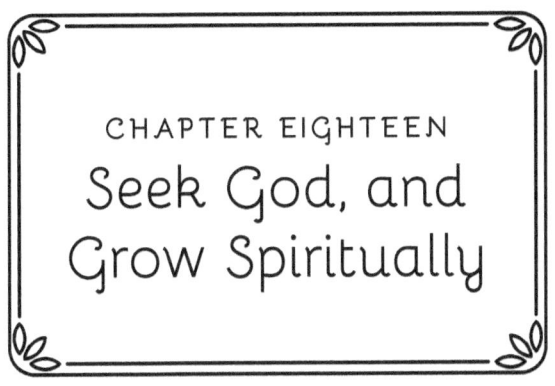

CHAPTER EIGHTEEN
Seek God, and Grow Spiritually

"Stay strong and keep the faith."
—Monsignor Richard J. Guastella (Father Rich)[19]

Lastly, and most importantly, with every opportunity and living breath, we must seek God, find God, and grow spiritually. Spirituality unites. Spirituality is about compassion, kindness, and love. The most important thing in life is to grow spiritually. Nothing should come before this—not family, friends, money, jobs, entertainment, materialistic items, or anything else. Use the *3 Ts: Talk* to God, *thank* God, *trust* God, and grow spiritually. Our relationship with God and our spiritual growth should be the most important parts of our lives. We experience life as human beings, however, we are spiritual beings. Speak, connect with and listen to God every day. Living a life close to God each day is the best life, especially since God is infinite and abundantly accessible to you. How you think and feel and what you say and do should bring honor and glory to God.

---

19 Affectionately remembered as "Father Rich"

CHOOSING TRUE HAPPINESS

Activate the power of God within you today, and start a new life today. Don't think you can do everything on your own, because that's not possible. With God, all things are possible. Without God, nothing is possible. You were created in the image and likeness of God. You are God's child. We are all God's children. I wish everybody on this Earth would realize once and for all that we are all God's children, part of one family, God's Family. God wants us to have a relationship with him. God wants to help us. Rely on God in every situation and all circumstances. You can't do it alone. And you don't *need* to because God is always by our side, and God always loves us. Consider living a Christ-centered life today.

God is our creator. Everything comes from God. Everything you see originated from God. Nothing in this world is separate from God. God is omnipresent, omniscient, omnipotent, and omnibenevolent. In other words, God is present everywhere, knows everything, has unlimited power, and is all good. Having faith and believing makes the invisible come to life. God is real, and heaven exists.

Spiritual growth means growing to know how God wants us to live so that we seek to please Him in all things. It is the process of becoming more and more like Jesus Christ. After salvation, every believer in Jesus begins the process of spiritual growth. When we place our faith in Jesus, the Holy Spirit begins the process of making us more like Him, conforming us to his image and likeness. With God's love, guidance, knowledge, and power, we have everything we need to live lives that bring honor and glory to God, which is the goal of spiritual growth. What we need comes through our knowledge of Him, which is the key to obtaining everything we need.

Our knowledge of Him comes from the Word, given to us for our spiritual growth and our intellectual and moral growth. Spiritual growth is a lifelong process that depends on our study and application of God's Word and our walk in the Spirit. As we seek spiritual growth, we should pray to God and ask for wisdom concerning the areas He desires us to grow in. We can ask God to increase our faith and knowledge of Him. God desires for us to grow spiritually, and He has given us all we need to experience spiritual growth.

SEEK GOD, AND GROW SPIRITUALLY

We have to press continually toward deeper knowledge of God in Christ. With the Holy Spirit's help, we can overcome sin and steadily become more like my Savior, the Lord Jesus Christ. Before speaking or acting, ask yourself, "What would Jesus do?" *WWJD?* Then make your choice. Strive to be Christ-like. Ask yourself, "How can I become more Christ-like?" Some days I live as Jesus did, and some days I fail miserably. However, in my mind and heart, Jesus Christ is number one in my life. Remember that spiritual growth is an ongoing process that will never end in this life.

Spiritual growth requires prioritizing. We need to change from pleasing ourselves to pleasing God and learning to obey God. We need to be consistent and show perseverance and do those things we know will bring us closer to God such as praying, studying the bible, following the Ten Commandments, and following Jesus's ways. God alone is our resource, and all growth comes by grace through Him, but we are responsible to make the choice to obey.

With God, all things are possible. God will get you through everything. God is involved in everything in your life. God has a plan and a purpose for you. You should ask God to direct your life and give you strength, courage, knowledge, and direction. Seek God, and God will give you strength, courage, knowledge, and direction. Also, remember to thank God for everything, especially all of your many blessings. Make sure you love God, serve God, and thank God. And know that God holds your future, just as He holds your past and present. You must first love God with all your mind, heart, and soul, and then love your neighbor as yourself. The most important relationship you will ever have is your relationship with God. We need to make choices that show we love God, ourselves, and others.

God shapes us through the events of our lives. If it is not going your way, it's okay—it's going God's way. All the trials and tribulations we face in our life are signs that God is guiding us. The obstacles are there to provide a learning experience. God does what's best for us and our spiritual growth. You may not understand it or see it at the moment, but, eventually, you will see and understand. Everything happens for a reason. Everything is meant to be. Trials and tribulations bring spiritual blessings. Also, God puts certain

CHOOSING TRUE HAPPINESS

people in your life at a certain time and for a certain reason. It's up to you to realize this. And remember God's love and forgiveness are always there to heal and strengthen us.

We need to be always present to the miracle of life. Each of us is an amazing creation of God. Stop and think about our beautiful God. What a great honor to be able to communicate and have a relationship with God, creator of heaven, Earth, and the entire universe.

I wish everybody here on this Earth would realize that we are all God's children, part of one family, God's family. We are all one. We are all connected. We have more in common than that which divides us. It is the thoughts, feelings, actions, opinions and selfishness of humans that divide us. That wasn't God's intent and plan for us. God wants us to have a relationship with him and love him, ourselves, and others.

We need to keep our minds focused on the things of God. Anything that encourages us to be loving, respectful, kind, compassionate, courageous, peaceful, just, patient, and pure is of God. When we focus on these things instead of the discouraging messages the world produces, we will produce them in our actions during our daily lives. Living in the current world, our minds can be distracted, influenced, and tempted by many different things. Don't let this happen to you; focus your mind on God. Don't fall into the terrible trap of just living and forgetting about God's existence.

We sin. God saves. Other things can wait, but the search for God cannot wait. How does God see you? God loves you more than you could ever understand—more in this present moment than anyone could in a lifetime. Try to see yourself through the eyes of God. And leave everything in God's hands; if you choose to do so, you will see amazing results. *God's gift to you is yourself.* What you end up making of yourself is your gift to God.

The focal point for many people in this world is their life here on Earth. What are my wants and desires? People's thoughts, words, and actions are related to what's good for them here on Earth. However, our life here on Earth is only for a limited time. Obviously, everybody knows that, but

SEEK GOD, AND GROW SPIRITUALLY

how often do people think about that? A lot of people are missing the big picture, which is eternal life. We need to start focusing more on our eternal life. According to mostimportantthing.org, eternal life is a life full, free, and forever. It is peace, joy, and assurance. It is comfort, strength, and hope. It is never-ending life with God in heaven after we die, but it's also abundant life here and now. Here are a couple of questions to reflect upon: Are you focusing on your earthly life or your eternal life? Will your earthly life lead you to eternal life?

> "The destination is a happy life, an accomplished life that doesn't end with death but with eternal life."
> —Angelo Scola (1)

> "Happy Moments, Praise God. Difficult Moments, Seek God. Quiet Moments, Worship God. Painful Moments, Trust God. Every Moment, Thank God."
> —Rick Warren (2)

> "To fall in love with God is the greatest romance; to seek him the greatest adventure; to find him, the greatest human achievement."
> —Saint Augustine (3)

> "God has a purpose for your pain, a reason for your struggle, and a reward for your faithfulness. Trust Him and don't give up."
> —Anonymous (4)

> "I know a lot of people struggle with the idea of Jesus and their idea of God. I think, if you don't even know what you're praying to or who you're praying to, based on what I know to be true, regardless, God's always listening."
> —Hailey Baldwin/Hailey Rhode Bieber (5)

CHOOSING TRUE HAPPINESS

"Jesus said, 'The Kingdom of God is within you.'"
—LUKE 17:21++[20]

"Jesus loves you. Jesus is your friend."
—MONSIGNOR RICHARD J. GUASTELLA (FATHER RICH)

---

[20] Why those 40 crosses? I was carrying my computer, a clipboard, and several other items from my dining room to my kitchen. When I put down the computer on my countertop, I noticed what looked like "addition signs." I had no idea how they got there. Then I realized I must have held down the shift button and pressed on the + sign at the same time, while I was carrying the computer and other items. I have no clue how that could have been possible. I decided to count the "addition signs" and what do you know? There were 40. I left them just as you see them. I realized that this was a sign from above and reinforced that God's hand is involved in this book. Also, it turns out that there are 40 chapters in this book. I never intended to use chapters, it just worked out like that. The number 40 represents many amazing events recorded in the bible.

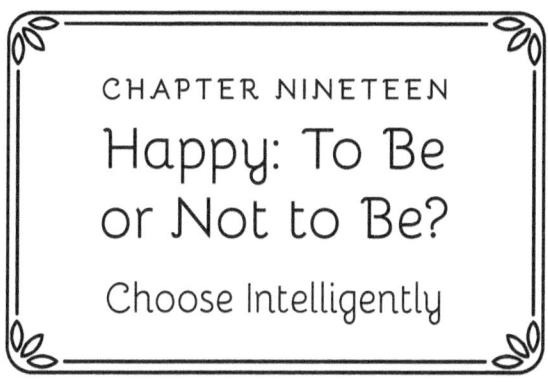

CHAPTER NINETEEN
Happy: To Be or Not to Be?
Choose Intelligently

"They don't make you what you are—you do.
You are what you choose to be."
—Harry Connick, Jr. (1)

Everything *starts with our thinking.* Positive thinking produces positive results. Negative thinking produces negative results. People become products of their thoughts; what they think, they become. Thoughts can be extremely powerful. Our thinking is directly connected to how we feel and act. We can change our emotions by changing our thinking. Let your mind be your best asset and most powerful tool.

Reflecting upon my experiences with anxiety and depression, I've come to the realization that I was mismanaging my thoughts and emotions. My thoughts and emotions were in charge of me. That's all anxiety and depression are—your thoughts and emotions working against you. You will experience true happiness and peace once you learn how to manage your thoughts and emotions. Make your thoughts and emotions work for you, not against you. It all starts with your thinking. Choose to have a disciplined mind. Train your mind to see the good in everything; positivity is a choice. True happiness in your life depends on the quality of your thoughts. We create our own stress, and it all starts with our thinking. In addition, it is our compulsive reaction to the situations in which we are placed that causes stress. Regardless of the situation, we always have the power to choose how we react. Through the years, I've learned to be more in charge of my thoughts and emotions. Learning to train my brain is a lifelong endeavor. It definitely takes a lot of practice. However, the time and effort to train your brain is well worth it.

In order to live a happy life, we must choose to do so. Happiness is a choice. Make your choices be based upon what truly matters and works. After we make the choice to be happy, our journey toward happiness may begin. We must really desire happiness and want it greatly. It takes determination and persistence to remain consistently and truly happy throughout your life. Ironically, happiness already lies within us. We are all created to be happy.

We have the capacity for self-awareness and are capable of helping ourselves. Unfortunately, people often neglect their mental, emotional, and physical health. Choosing to do so is a recipe for disaster. *Pleeeeease* spend a lot more time on self-care. As Agnes Wainman explained, self-care is "something that refuels us, rather than takes from us." Do you take care of yourself? In what ways do you take care of yourself?

Spend more time self-reflecting and less time criticizing and judging. Take a look in the mirror before you criticize or judge someone else. If you choose to judge and criticize, then start with yourself. If you choose to give compliments and encouragement, then start with others. Self-reflection can provide us with the answers that we need. Self-reflection can assess our strengths and weaknesses and help us reach our full potential. Self-reflection can help us learn more about ourselves, help us grow, and maybe even teach us something new about ourselves.

If you find yourself giving too much attention and focus to a situation that is bothering you, then perhaps you can use one of these three suggestions.

HAPPY: TO BE OR NOT TO BE? CHOOSE INTELLIGENTLY

1. Remove yourself from the situation
2. Change the situation
3. Totally accept the situation

Focus on things you can control. Accept things you can't control.

If we don't truly know ourselves, we might not be able to help ourselves. However, if change needs to occur, we have to take responsibility for our words and actions. And that might start with the fact of acknowledging that we need to change. Some people change, while others choose not to change. If people choose not to change, you can't save them from themselves. You can't help people who don't want to help themselves. Sometimes we have to accept people for who they are. And accepting them for who they are may be quite the challenge, especially if who they are is not someone you want them to be. Currently, when it comes to dealing with my dad's life, I still struggle to accept him for who he is and what he has done with his life. And what he continues to do with his life. It's a hard pill to swallow.

Change is the only constant in our life. After you acknowledge that you need to change, the next step is recognizing what it is you want to change. Try to notice when you repeat negative thought patterns or negative habits. Choose to embrace change, and run with it. You'll never know what could have been unless you make the change. Change can lead to new opportunities and a better life. Change can help you grow and challenge you. It can make you stronger. Whenever one door closes, another one opens. However, you will not be able to open the new door unless you close the old one. If necessary, slam the old door shut! Everyone has the free will and power to change their thinking, words, feelings, choices, actions, and attitudes. As Mahatma Gandhi said, "You must be the change that you wish to see in the world."

Change is healthy and a big part of life. If you resist change, you resist life. Adapt, adjust, and keep moving forward. Make the best of the current situation. Do the best that you can with what you have and where you are. I highly recommend reading, *Who Moved My Cheese?* by Spencer Johnson. It's a great book that helped me deal with change in my life. It can also help you deal with change in all aspects of your life.

Accept the people in your life for who they are, not for who you want them to be. Try to find some good in people, and focus on their positive qualities. You don't need to fix the people you interact with. Resign from being the savior. I had to learn this the hard way with my father's life. God is the savior, not you. Your role is to bring honor and glory to God in how you think, how you feel, what you say, and what you do. Everybody needs to learn on their own. It's important for people to suffer the fullest consequences of their choices and actions. Everybody is responsible for their own life.

A sense of belonging is the feeling of being connected and accepted as a member or part. It is a powerful change agent for redirecting negative behavior. A sense of belonging is a basic and very important human need. It can be so powerful that it can create both value in life *and* the ability to learn healthy coping skills when experiencing intensive and painful emotions. Finding ways to belong can help ease any negative emotions.

How can we create a sense of belonging? Some find connection and belonging with family, friends, peers, work, school, church, sports, groups, and clubs.

Building a sense of belonging requires effort and practice. One way to work on increasing your sense of belonging is to focus on and look for commonalities you have with others. Another way is to work on acceptance of others. To accept others and views that are not the same as yours requires keeping an open mind and respecting other people's thoughts, feelings, ideas, opinions and perspectives.

A great way to communicate acceptance is through validation. Validation is recognizing or affirming that a person or their feelings or opinions are valid or worthwhile. Validation strengthens relationships and builds a sense of belonging. Validation is the acknowledgment that someone's thoughts and feelings are understandable; it helps you stay on the same side, with a sense of belonging, even when you disagree.

Be aware of your thinking, words, and actions—especially the thoughts that you frequently think. Also, take notice of what things you identify with most and what words you use to describe something.

HAPPY: TO BE OR NOT TO BE? CHOOSE INTELLIGENTLY

Through your thoughts, what you say, and what you do, you are either creating togetherness or separateness. There are "me people" and there are "we people." The *me* people are all about *I, I, I*. The *we* people are all about *us, us, us*. Choose to be part of the "we people."

It's important for people to feel connected to one another and connected to what they do on a daily basis. Togetherness is an important aspect of life. It unites us, gives us security, much-needed support, and a sense of belonging—to an organization, a greater community, or team. Togetherness improves our levels of determination and motivation, mental health, and happiness. When you see your connection to others, you realize that all people face difficulties and struggles during their lifetime.

Everybody has a story. And everybody has a "me, too" story. You are not alone. You are *never* alone—and this should be comforting to know. After all, we are all human, and nobody is perfect; everybody makes mistakes. As human beings, we are obligated to consciously do the best we can for everyone and everything we encounter in our lives and come in touch with. We are all in this together. Along the journey, we will all make mistakes. I've made a lot of mistakes, especially between the ages of 14 to 24. I'm human; we're human. Please don't repeat your mistakes, as often as I have. You can learn valuable lessons from your mistakes. You should learn from your mistakes rather than repeat them. This took me quite some time to really understand and learn regarding certain people and situations in my life. Specifically, dealing with and accepting my father's life. He was hurting and disappointing me so much with the way he was living his life, especially with the compulsive gambling and drinking. Nevertheless, for many years I continued to make him my priority. I desperately wanted him to change. With great hope, I tried numerous times to help him, but my efforts were to no avail. The bottom line was he never wanted to help himself. The hard lesson that I had to learn was you can't help people who don't want to help themselves. That may be difficult to accept, but that was the reality of the situation. Now I say to myself, "It is what it is." Another mistake I made was waiting way too long to reach out for help when I was feeling depressed. It was hard for me to ask for help. I was holding everything in. Please don't let this happen to you. I should've gotten help much sooner. Please learn from my mistakes. If you are feeling depressed or anxious, please reach out for help immediately. Getting help for yourself and/or others is a sign of honesty, intelligence, strength, and courage. Don't let another day go by without getting the help that you need. You got this. You can do it!

Each and every human being has something special and unique about them. All of us have some type of skill and talent. I believe all of us are born with special qualities, abilities, skills, and talents. The sooner we explore and make these discoveries, the more time we have to develop these qualities, abilities, skills, and talents. It will take a lot of patience, practice, and persistence to develop these qualities, abilities, skills, and talents to the fullest. Look for opportunities to do so, and take advantage of these opportunities. Focus on your strengths, not your weaknesses. You will increase your happiness level by identifying, stating, and focusing on your strengths. Remember, all of our lives have purpose and meaning. Find your purpose and meaning. Those who are happiest feel they are contributing to something good, worthwhile, and important: the greater good.

There is neither past nor future (in being); there is only the present. Yesterday was the present when you experienced it; tomorrow will also be the present when you experience it. Therefore, experience takes place only in the present, and beyond and apart from experience (being in the present moment), nothing exists. Realize that the past and future don't exist. The only thing we really have and that truly exists is the present moment. When do you think of a memory? In the present moment. When do you think of something that *could* happen? In the present moment. See? Only the present moment exists, nothing else.

Be present every day. The only thing there is, ever was, and ever will be is the present moment. The "past" is done, the "future" is not here yet—only the present moment/now exists. Try to focus, concentrate, and live in the present moment. Seize the present moment, the present second, the present minute, the present hour, the present day. Cherish the present moment. There are many beautiful moments that are missed because some people aren't aware of the present moment. The present moment is a gift—that's why it's called *the present*.

So much of a person's life can zip by without them really enjoying and getting the most out of the present moment. That's a real shame. Don't let this happen to you. Stop and take a slow, deep, focused breath, and enjoy the present moment. It's all that we have. Learn to live in the present moment. Life can be lived and experienced only in the moment.

> In any given moment, continuing to remain present does require awareness—of when your thoughts are not present or when you are being judgmental of your situation or surroundings, or your mind is elsewhere.[21]

A lot of unhappiness can be attributed to people living in the "past" or worrying about the "future." *There's no such thing as past and future—they simply don't exist.* Only the present moment exists. The "past" is done—forget about it and move on. Leave the "past" where it belongs, behind you. The "future" is not here yet. So why worry about it? Most of the things we worry about don't happen, anyway. So, don't waste your time and energy worrying about them. Fear is always about that which is not yet or is never going to be. Fear is mostly useless and self-destructive mind activity. Every fearful thought about the "future" is about something that *could or may* happen. Why create fear for yourself over something that hasn't happened?

Worrying is a big waste of valuable time and energy. Don't be afraid or worrisome; eventually, everything falls into place. Everything has a way of working itself out. The moment you recognize a fearful thought for what it is—your mind working against you and creating brain farts—you begin not to identify with the

---

21 *5 Key Steps to Finding True Happiness and Peace, According to Zen Buddhism*, by the Power of Ideas in Mind, Body, Philosophy, and Culture http://thepowerofideas.ideapod.com/5-key-finding-true-happiness-peace-according-zen-buddhism

CHOOSING TRUE HAPPINESS

fear. Worry and fear pretend to be necessary, but they have no useful purpose. Worry and fear are just our minds tricking us and wasting our time and energy.

If you choose to think about the "past"—of course, in the present moment—let it be for a beautiful memory or for a learning experience, perhaps helping yourself or learning from a mistake. These are the main reasons you should be visiting the "past." If you choose to think about the "future"—of course, in the present moment—let it be for planning or achieving goals. Focus on the present moment, and enjoy it to the fullest. The present moment is the only thing that exists. Remember, our thoughts keep trying to pull us to the "past" and "future." Therefore, you may need to keep redirecting yourself to the present moment, but it will be well worth it. Every day I keep redirecting my thoughts constantly by taking a slow, deep, focused breath and listening to the sound of my breath.

> All there really *is* is a present moment, and that the past and the future are merely concepts that are useful to the mind.[22]

> Simply ignore all unwelcome thoughts and carry on with your day—blissfully uninvolved with egoic thought, mindfully engaged only with the present-moment awareness of the here and now. As your attention onto egoic thought fades, so, too, will the ego itself.

> Realize that there is no intention, cause, or purpose behind any thought. Do not read anything into them whatsoever.[23]

---

[22] *Is the Present Moment Really the Only Thing That Exists?* by Colton Tanner Casados-Medve. https://medium.com/@radioren-7/is-the-present-moment-really-the-only-thing-that-exists-18ce550800ee

[23] ZEN THINKING *July 05, 2016* "Learning to Not Indulge the Egoic Mind," by Brian Thompson, http://www.zenthinking.net/blog/learning-to-not-indulge-the-egoic-mind

HAPPY: TO BE OR NOT TO BE? CHOOSE INTELLIGENTLY

Love is something we all need and desire. It is what we can give the most to make a difference in the world. It brings out the best in us. Love is one of the most powerful forces in the universe. The power of love is extraordinary: It leads us to the power of miracles. You are a miracle.

Here's the order of love:

* God
* Yourself
* Family/Pets
* Friends
* Others
* Any living things

Love is the most powerful emotion of all. Love is one's constant inner state. Love is extremely empowering. One of the greatest gifts in this world is love. Love conquers all. Always remember you are loved beyond belief. Live the life that you love, and love the life that you live. And don't forget to be loving, respectful, kind and compassionate to yourself and others.

Each day, a focal point in your life should be becoming a better human being. Trying to become a good or better human being is a noble and noteworthy endeavor. Believe it or not, there is goodness in everyone. It's just a question of finding it and allowing it to emerge. Be the best person that you can be each and every day. Be your best self. Try to be a better person today than you were yesterday. Everybody has room for improvement. Being a kind human being is a great legacy to leave behind.

Forgiveness is a conscious, deliberate decision to release feelings of resentment or vengeance toward a person or group who has harmed you, regardless of whether they actually deserve your forgiveness. Forgiveness does not mean forgetting, nor does it mean condoning or excusing offenses. Forgiveness is an act of the will. Forgiveness is a deliberate act of love, mercy, and grace.

CHOOSING TRUE HAPPINESS

Forgiveness is a choice. It can consist of forgiving yourself, a person or a group. Forgiveness is liberating and powerful. It can make you feel free, allowing you to do the right thing. Forgiveness brings the forgiver peace of mind and frees them from destructive anger. It is in our own best interest to forgive. Forgiveness is for our own growth and happiness. When we hold onto hurt, pain, anger, and resentment, it harms us far more than it harms the offender. Don't hold onto anger or any other negative emotion. You are only hurting yourself by staying angry. *Anger is a wind that blows out the light of the mind.* If you choose to remain angry, then you are allowing your mind to be in charge.

I know personally that it can be challenging and difficult to let go of your anger, however, be wise and courageous, and don't let those negative feelings win. Challenge yourself to a game. If those feelings of anger, resentment, or vengeance persist, then you lose. If those feelings of anger, resentment, or vengeance dissipate, then you win. Win the game! There have been some days that I've won the game and some days that I've lost the game. Currently, most days I'm hoping to win the game.

Do you want someone you are upset and angry with to control your emotions? Well, that's what you're doing when you don't forgive someone and hold grudges. Until you forgive someone who has wronged you, you allow that person to have power over you.

Someone I really needed to forgive in my life is my dad. It was very difficult, because I wasn't letting go of my disappointment, hurt, frustration, and anger. It took a lot of time. However, I made the right choice and decided to forgive him for his many mistakes. Do you really want a person you are upset, hurt by, frustrated, and angry with to have power over you?

Forgiveness frees us to live in the present moment. Forgiveness allows us to move on without anger, contempt, or seeking revenge. There is no revenge as powerful and complete as forgiveness. There's a person, a couple, and a group you must forgive. The person is yourself. The couple is your parents. And the group is everybody else. Be your

HAPPY: TO BE OR NOT TO BE? CHOOSE INTELLIGENTLY

own teammate. Don't beat yourself up. Remember we are all human beings, and everybody makes mistakes. Nobody is perfect.

The time to forgive yourself for your mistakes is right now. First you need to admit that you made mistakes. It takes courage to admit that you have done something wrong. The time to forgive others for their mistakes is also right now. Forgiveness is a decision not to hold something against another person or group, despite what has been done to you. Do not hold grudges. Grudges are unhealthy for everybody. Everyone makes mistakes. If you can't forgive others, don't expect others to forgive you. Forgive, and you will be forgiven. Think forgiveness. There's always the power of hope, help, faith, prayer, love, and, of course, forgiveness. Forgive others not because they deserve forgiveness, but because you deserve peace.

The "f" word, ugh . . ." I am speaking about forgiveness. We all want forgiveness and the release it can bring to our lives and to our hearts. It's not hard to say—it is hard to make it stick. For me, it was the Oprah Winfrey show that was my forgiveness "aha" moment. To forgive is not to condone the act done by whoever, but to release the hurt, pain, resentment, and anger that lives in our heart, mind, and soul.
Want to be free of those feelings that are holding you down? Follow these seven steps to release the emotions of hurt, pain, resentment, and anger, and set your heart and soul free.

1. **Identify the Act**
   What exactly is it you need to forgive?
   Write down in as much detail as possible

what you keep holding onto. What is it that you cannot let go?

2. **The Emotions**
   Emotions drive us to hold onto things. How did this make you feel? How do you feel today about it? Be as specific as you can with the emotions that come up every time you relive this act. If you need to, sit quiet for a few minutes connecting with your breath, and let the emotions come to the surface.

3. **The Person Responsible**
   Who is this person? What is your relationship like now? What were the circumstances involving this act? Write it down with as much description and honesty as you can.

4. **Your Participation**
   What was your participation in this? That's not implying that you caused it, but rather asking why you didn't stop it. Why didn't you protect yourself? Do not blame yourself—that is not the direction to go. We all participate in things that happen in our lives, and sometimes in order to fully forgive someone, we must also forgive ourselves for our participation.

5. **Changing the Future**
   What will it look like when all this is

released? How will you feel? What will the interaction be like with this person? What will your day look like with this release of emotions and the healing that will come?

6. **Forgiveness**
   Write a letter to this person, forgiving them for whatever happened. Tell them why you are forgiving them. Do not forget to forgive yourself as well. Do not be accusatory—just be honest about the impact this incident had on your life. Explain how forgiving them will continue to change your life in a healthy way.

7. **The Release**
   Take this letter and all your notes, and have a ceremony. Burn them, cut them into tiny pieces, and throw them away. Put them in water and let them dissolve. Say a mantra of forgiveness such as, "I forgive you; I heal by forgiving myself and letting love back into my heart." Do not forget to include praise for yourself. This is not easy sometimes, but if you wish to have peace in your soul, then these steps will certainly get you there. You are now released from bringing this up anymore, it is gone, it is released, and you are free from it.
   Bravo to you for honoring yourself. Take

some time to be proud of the hard work
you have just worked through. May your
life be filled with love and light.[24]

For anyone who wants to learn something about forgiveness, look to the life of Scarlett Lewis.

Scarlett is teaching many children and adults all over the world that they have the power to choose a loving thought over an angry thought, and, in turn, create a more peaceful world. What an extraordinary—and successful—mission Scarlett is implementing in the world.

The Story Behind the Movement

Scarlett founded the Choose Love Movement after her son, Jesse, was murdered during the Sandy Hook Elementary School tragedy in December 2012. It is one of the worst mass shootings in U.S. history.

At six years old, Jesse, alongside 19 of his beloved, first-grade classmates and six, beloved educators, died. Yet law enforcement says Jesse used his final moments to heroically save nine of his friends. Shortly after his death, Scarlett decided to be part of the solution to the issues that we're seeing in our society today—and that also caused the tragedy. She created the Choose Love Movement and became an advocate for character development and social and emotional learning (SEL), which teaches children how to manage their emotions, feel connected, and have healthy relationships.

Before his death, Jesse left a message on their kitchen chalkboard, "Norturting Helinn Love." (Nurturing, Healing, Love). When Scarlett learned that these words are included in the definition of "compassion" across all cultures, she realized that love, connection, and belonging are universal wants and needs that connect all of

---

[24] *Seven Steps to Forgiveness*, by Janine Reed Oct 31, 2016 · 3 min. read https://medium.com/@reedj_99876/seven-steps-to-forgiveness-866b91687f52

HAPPY: TO BE OR NOT TO BE? CHOOSE INTELLIGENTLY

humanity. With the guidance of Christopher Kukk, PhD, Dean of the Cormier Honors College for Citizen Scholars and Professor of Political Science at Longwood University, a Fulbright Scholar and author of, The Compassionate Achiever, these three words led to the creation of a formula that can be used by anyone, at any time, anywhere in the world to manage their response to any situation.

The Choose Love Formula™ is:
Courage + Gratitude + Forgiveness + Compassion in Action = Choosing Love

These four character values are easy to learn. When practiced, they strengthen the health and resilience of individuals, improve the community and culture of groups, and promote a safer, more peaceful and loving world.

Jesse Lewis Choose Love Movement™ began as a no-cost program for schools but has organically expanded into programs for home, for work, and for community. Sports teams are using the Choose Love programs to teach leadership. Prisons use it for restoration. Even military families are using it to ease anxiety and strengthen relationships.

Since 2013, The Jesse Lewis Choose Love Movement has been on a mission to create safer schools and a safer world by teaching people how to use nurturing, healing love in any circumstance. Practicing social and emotional learning skills improves culture and cultivates an environment that is welcoming, supportive, compassionate, and safe.

Jesse Lewis Choose Love Movement™ is a 501(c)(3) nonprofit organization with a mission to create safer and more loving communities through groundbreaking, next-generation social and emotional learning (SEL) programs that are free of cost and suited for all stages of life.

The programs offered are tailored for any age from toddlers through adulthood. At the core of it all is a simple formula—**Courage**

CHOOSING TRUE HAPPINESS

+ Gratitude + Forgiveness + Compassion in Action = Choosing Love—that anyone can learn and practice to improve the world around them.

The Choose Love Formula™ is the foundation of the next generation of Social and Emotional Learning and Character Education programming that was originally created for schools but has quickly spread into homes, communities, and the workplace to strengthen connection and promote a more peaceful, loving world.[25]

Scarlett has taught me that if she can forgive the assassin of her six-year-old son, Jesse, then I can forgive any person or situation in my life. Furthermore, Scarlett has developed understanding and compassion for the culprit. Absolutely amazing and astonishing!!! What a remarkable human being!

Jesse has taught me that I have the power to choose how I respond in any circumstance. Also, he has made me realize that I have a tremendous amount of courage. Jesse Lewis = Ultimate Courage.

In addition, Jesse has reminded me how truly precious time is and not to waste it. And, finally, Jesse has helped me to be a more loving person.

Both Scarlett and Jessie have inspired me and helped me to realize that regardless of the circumstance, you can always Choose Love! I don't know a better message than that.

Scarlett and I have a dream to see the Choose Love Movement implemented in as many schools and places as possible in the United States and throughout the world. It's free and definitely effective. And what better message can you spread than LOVE???

Moderation and self-control are key components to living a happy life. Avoid excesses and extremes, and live with moderation. Drinking and eating foods in moderation are keys to maintaining a healthy diet and lifestyle.

Show restraint and discipline in your thoughts, words and actions. Even good things can become obstacles to us if used without moderation.

---

25 https://chooselovemovement.org

HAPPY: TO BE OR NOT TO BE? CHOOSE INTELLIGENTLY

Instead of having three scoops of ice cream, have one. Don't keep eating until you're super full. Instead of speaking too much, start listening more often. Currently, I'm practicing listening more and speaking less. Instead of listening to, following, and believing negative thoughts, ignore them, laugh at them, or replace them with positive thoughts. Instead of thinking so much, try to take a slow, deep, focused breath and concentrate on the present moment, and think less.

Moderation avoids extremes, exercises restraint, and is related to self-control. Moderation is a great thing, but living a life of moderation can be quite the challenge. We need to learn and understand that excesses and extremes are unhealthy and don't work well for us or provide us with true happiness. The only area of your life that moderation doesn't apply to is God.

It is God's gift to enjoy one's life and His gifts. However, to value those things more than God leaves us still desiring what our hearts really need first and foremost—Him.

What does the bible say about moderation?

Practicing moderation is a good discipline.

In fact, self-control is one of the qualities that the Holy Spirit produces in the life of a believer. When we are not living in moderation—when we lack self-control in a certain area of our lives—it can indicate that we're not allowing God fully into that area. We need not live in defeat. God does not condemn His children, and we have been granted the victory over every sin. Plus, the spirit wants to give us self-control. When we surrender to God as "living sacrifices," He will meet the needs that we're trying to satisfy on our own. The sheep that follow the Good Shepherd will "lack nothing."

The world appeals to the lust of the flesh and advances the lie that what we need is more pleasure, more stuff, more entertainment, etc. What we really need more of is God. God designed us to need and desire Him above all else. All other things must be in moderation.

CHOOSING TRUE HAPPINESS

The only area in which we don't need to be concerned about moderation is God Himself. We are to love God without limits. We can never have too much of God, and we can never love him too much. And the more we ask him to fill us and invade our lives with His Holy Spirit, the easier it becomes to live in moderation in all other things. Choose moderation. All things in moderation, except God.[26]

Make the choice to be in charge of your own life. Don't let other people or events take you off course. You are in charge of your life, not others. Don't let other people or things direct your life. You be the director. We can control what we say, what we do, how we react, and what our attitude will be. We can't control what other people say, what other people do, how others react, or the attitude of others. Don't stress over things that we can't control. After learning many valuable lessons through the years, one of my favorite things now to say or think is, "Just wait and see, whatever will be will be."

Utilize your precious time intelligently; be productive. Pace yourself—slow and steady wins the race. Stay focused and persistent until you experience favorable outcomes. Work on goals every day; eventually, you'll get there. It's not where you are standing—it's what direction you are moving in. Keep your eye on the prize. Don't make excuses. Excuses just keep you in your own little circle. Set attainable and SMART GOALS to strive for, and don't stop until you get there. Make sure you are moving in the right direction. You have the power to choose your own direction. You have the power to take charge of your life. Our lives are shaped by the choices that we make. Our choices define who we are and what we become. Sometimes people don't have the knowledge and courage to make the choices that they need to fulfill their destiny. It takes courage to grow up and be who you really are meant to be. It takes courage to live your life the way you want to. You have more courage than you could ever imagine. Courage is fear turned inside out.

---

26 **What does the Bible say about moderation?** https://www.gotquestions.org/Bible-moderation.html

HAPPY: TO BE OR NOT TO BE? CHOOSE INTELLIGENTLY

I do believe we all have a purpose and a destiny, however, you need to make good choices in order to fulfill your purpose and destiny. Along the path of life here on Earth, we will all face struggles at one point or another in our lives. Struggle brings strength. There will be challenges. Rise to the challenge. What doesn't kill us makes us stronger. Our trials and tribulations can mold us and lead us on a better path. Without the darkness there will be no light. We must go through the darkness in order to find the light. It's our moments of struggle that define us and shape who we become. How we choose to respond to these struggles is what matters.

It's during difficult times that we can grow, become stronger, and develop impeccable character. Ultimately, perseverance should prevail, because we are all much stronger than we think we are and much braver than we can ever imagine. Be determined and persistent. Determination and persistence will conquer most things. Everyone has a story—make yours a great one.

We all need to be very aware and keep our eyes open. Things are not always as they seem. Sometimes, we have to look for the deeper meaning, the silver lining. Every cloud has a silver lining. Everything happens for a reason. Follow your intuition and inner guidance. Listen and follow your hunches. Be in tune and very aware of everything that is happening around you. You meet certain people in your life, at certain times, for certain reasons. I believe some events in our lives that we may perceive as coincidences are not *really* "coincidences." These events, circumstances, and experiences happen for a reason.

I wish everyone would realize we are all God's Children, part of One Family, God's Family. We are all one. All *in* the same race and *part* of the same race, the human race. We all bleed red and are the same on the inside. See yourself in others. We are all human beings living on this Earth together. Albert Einstein told us that "Everything is energy"; that "a human being is a part of the whole called by us [the] Universe."

Our differences make life special and unique. Our similarities show we are all human, all one. We all should be treating one another with love, respect, kindness and compassion. A big part of being compassionate is realizing our shared humanity. When people are compassionate toward one another, it makes the world a better place. We all should be able to co-exist in peace and harmony. If we all constantly practiced expressing love, respect, kindness, and compassion to the ones around us, then we would experience a deeper sense of peace and happiness. And you never know what somebody is going through in their life. Therefore, be kind and respectful when interacting with people.

Instead, some humans choose to dominate and mistreat one another, causing conflict, violence, chaos, poverty, and power struggles. A person's religion, race, and nationality are just a part of their identity. Yet, the religion, race, and nationality of people produce such unnecessary conflict and violence. Why? *The works of the egoic mind.* The world is the way it is because *that's the way people made it.*

There is a desperate need for a change and shift in human behavior and understanding that allows there to be true peace on Earth. We can change the world, one person at a time. Everybody needs to start with the person in the mirror. It is much more difficult to judge oneself than to judge others. Nevertheless, we can find the strength, courage, and energy within ourselves to make the appropriate changes. Some people choose to change, while others choose not to change. Remember—everything is one energy, and everything is one. Try to find some good in all things. Live your life focusing on the positive, not focusing on the negative. Focus on the solution, not on the problem. Be part of the solution, not part of the problem. We all can live in harmony and peace if we all choose to do so. What are you doing to make the world a better place? How do your thoughts, feelings, words, and actions impact the lives of other people?

The most important relationship that you will ever have in your life is your relationship with God. I believe you can have a personal relationship with God through Jesus Christ. Jesus said, "I am the way and the truth and the life. No one comes to the Father except through me." This is my favorite bible quote, John 14:6. Your relationship with God should come first and foremost above all other relationships in your life. When you have a personal relationship with God, God can help guide you through anything. God is our God forever, and he will be our guide even to the end. There is no relationship of greater importance. There is no part of life more important than to know God and be in a relationship with God. There is no greater and more important relationship than with God.

HAPPY: TO BE OR NOT TO BE? CHOOSE INTELLIGENTLY

We grow our relationship with God through prayer, which should be consistent, constant, and committed. All things we are to take to God in prayer, recognizing that he is our source of love, strength, courage, and direction. Put everything in God's hands. Depend on God in every situation. Realize that God is our rock, our source of life, and the most important relationship of all. We were created in the image of God, with worth and value. God wants what's best for us, and God knows what's best for us. During mass, Father Patrick, a former priest at my parish, St. Clare's, would say, "God is good," and then the parishioners would respond, "All the time." Then Father Patrick would say, "All the time," and the parishioners answered, "God is good."

God wants our life to count and have meaning and purpose. God loves you more than you could ever imagine; nothing can separate you from God's love. God wants to have a personal relationship with you. Make your relationship with God the most important and powerful relationship in your life. With God all things are possible. Without God, nothing is possible. Where do you find yourself at this moment?

1. I don't have, and I don't want to have, a personal relationship with God through Jesus Christ.
2. I don't have, but I would like to have a personal relationship with God through Jesus Christ.
3. I do have a saving, personal relationship with God through Jesus Christ.

Whatever number you choose—1, 2, or 3—is your choice. However, I think choice three will give you the best life. You need to decide that for yourself. I encourage you, as I did, to research the facts about the life of Jesus. Perhaps your spiritual journey will begin and continue to grow. My spiritual journey began by praying, connecting to nature, researching the facts about Jesus' life, and reading about near-death experiences. Try to grow spiritually and find your God zone in your own way. And please strive to have a great relationship with God in a way that works for you. One of the main purposes of this book is to help you grow spiritually and find your own God zone.

CHOOSING TRUE HAPPINESS

God is the answer. God is freedom. God is omnipresent—He is everywhere. God is omnipotent—He has unlimited power. God is omniscient—He knows everything. God is omnibenevolent—He is all-good. Give God the honor and glory he desires and deserves. Our main purpose is to serve God. Love God with all your mind, heart, and soul. Love your neighbor as yourself. After all, we are all God's children, part of one family, God's family. It should be an honor to be part of God's great big family.

You were born by his purpose and for his purpose. We gain our value and validation in God and God alone. It is my heartfelt wish and great hope that one day all human beings will realize that we are all God's Children, part of one family, God's family. And how you think, how you feel, what you say, and what you do should bring glory and honor to God, reflect that you follow God's Word, and are part of God's family.

When God created the Earth, he didn't want all the land and natural resources to be conquered and divided. God's intention was for all his children to share and enjoy the beautiful land and amazing natural resources. There's plenty for everybody. If only all humans would realize this. If only everybody would work together. If only all humans would see God's true intention for his children. Mother Earth is a beautiful place and belongs to all that inhabit it. It's certain people that ruin this world.

Mother Earth should always come before money. Furthermore, the best interest of human beings is and always will be more important than the best interest of money. People should always come before money. Unfortunately, in the world we live in, money comes before people and Mother Earth. The love of money and the need for power are the roots to most evil.

We all should choose true happiness in our lives. Out with the negative and in with the positive! But happiness isn't something that just happens to you. There are steps to follow in order to be happy.

Here are five key steps that lead to long-term happiness.

1. We must want to be happy.
2. We need to accept guidance to achieve this.

HAPPY: TO BE OR NOT TO BE? CHOOSE INTELLIGENTLY

3. We need to apply self-discipline in order to follow the guidance.
4. We need to shift the focus to making inner, not outer, changes.
5. We need truly to accept that both happiness and unhappiness are choices we make.[27]

How to Be Happy in 7 Steps

Here are the seven steps:

Step 1: Happiness is a choice

Happiness is determined by how much we appreciate and enjoy what we have. Happy people make the best of everything. When we grow up, we all have the opportunity to be in charge of our life and be happy, regardless of where we were born and what kind of childhood we had. Happy people focus on what they have; unhappy people focus on what they don't have. If you are unhappy with your life, changes must be made. You can't keep doing the same thing over and over and expect different results. Change is good. Don't get stuck in a rut and/or become complacent. Let the hard times make you stronger, the mistakes make you smarter, and the sad experiences make you happier. You can be a happy person and live a happy life.

Happiness is a choice. You need to understand that we can choose to be happy or choose not to be happy. Luckily, we can choose how we want to live our life. Whatever the circumstances are, the choice is ours. Choose happiness or misery—it's up to you.

"If you can once really grasp that happiness is a choice, you will have learned one of the most important lessons of all existence."[28]

True happiness comes from within. It is not something that depends on what other people say or do. It depends on you and only you. You can choose

---

27 *Five Essential Steps to Happiness* April 21, 2016, by Nayaswami Jyotish https://www.ananda.org/jyotish-and-devi/five-essential-steps-happiness/
28 *Five Essential Steps to Happiness*—Nayaswamis Jyotish and Devi http:www.jyotishanddevi.org/touch-of-light/five-essential-steps-happiness

CHOOSING TRUE HAPPINESS

happiness today and be in charge of how you feel and not let your thoughts and emotions be in charge of you. However, the first crucial step is to really make up your mind to be happy.

Happiness will not be part of your life until you choose to be happy. Happiness must be a very important priority in your life. The more important happiness is to you, the happier times you will have in your life. You can start to be happy at any moment you want, even right at this moment. What you need to do is make a choice and choose to be happy. You can use a simple daily positive affirmation like, "Starting right now, I am going to be a happy person."

Once you make the choice to be a happy person, your journey may begin. You must be prepared to do whatever it takes to be happy. Turn your happiness on, and *keep* it on. So, if you make a choice to live a happy life, no matter what life brings you, it is more likely you will have a happy life because this is what you want, and you will not accept anything else. Make the choice to be happy, and stick to it. You can be happy during any time in your life, regardless of your circumstances. Instead of wallowing in misery, be happy. You have to understand that happiness is a choice and comes from within. It is never too late to choose a life of happiness—better late than never. Unfortunately, too many people have thrown in the towel and given up on happiness. Don't choose to accept an unhappy life. Fight on, and never, ever give up or quit. Every situation provides an opportunity to be well or suffer—the choice is ours. If you know how to be at ease within yourself, every situation is an opportunity.

Let happiness be a choice that you are willing to make and commit to. This choice will probably be the most important step toward becoming happy. Take a good, deep look at yourself: Realize the things that make you happy and the things that do not make you happy. Appreciate wholeheartedly the things that make you happy. From the moment I wake up in the morning, I watch my feet hit the floor and I say to myself, "Thank you, God, for another day." Keep a positive mindset and attitude toward your day from the moment you wake up until the end of your day. At the end of my day, before I go to bed, I say my prayers and once again thank God for another day. Studies show that

HAPPY: TO BE OR NOT TO BE? CHOOSE INTELLIGENTLY

a person can greatly affect their perspective in life by changing their attitudes and mindsets about things.

Happiness is often elusive, but it's desired by everyone. We spend much of our lives chasing happiness. Happiness is a choice you have to commit to. Nothing good in life comes easy, especially happiness. Happiness is a choice that you can decide on in a split second. However, achieving it takes some time and effort. Happiness is a choice that centers around how you handle yourself in your current environment.

Always show appreciation and be grateful; don't take things for granted. Help as many people as you can, and be as generous as possible, whether the need is spiritual, emotional, or material. You never know: At another time, *you* could be the one in need.

Don't try to take control of things that you can't control. Every day, there are a lot of little, free things that can put a smile on your face and in your heart and brighten up your day. For example, every day I try to connect with nature—whether it's admiring the sky and clouds or looking at trees or the sun or watching birds. You can make the choice right now to be happy. The choice is yours, happiness or unhappiness.

Step 2: Happiness is an attitude of mind

When you change the way you look at things, the things that you look at change. You will start feeling happier when you change your thinking, perspective, and attitude toward challenges and life itself. If you change the way you look at challenging situations, then those challenging situations change. You need to change your thinking, attitude, and perspective. Remember—nobody has a problem-free life; nobody gets a free ride.

You see, *the problem is not really the problem*. The problem is your thinking, perspective, and attitude about the problem. It's how we think about and react to the problem that creates our frame of mind and state of mind. You want to have a positive mind frame and be in a good state of mind as much as possible. You choose; you are in charge. Don't let your mind focus and dwell on "problems." Instead, spend the time and effort to find a solution.

CHOOSING TRUE HAPPINESS

There's always a solution to the "problem." Just make a plan, stick to it, and solve it. Just do it. Don't overthink, overanalyze, overcomplicate, and/or overreact. While we are in the middle of a difficult situation, it often feels as though it's never going to change. That's because your mind is tricking you and lying to you. Don't get tricked and believe the lies. Instead, think to yourself, "This, too, shall pass." When I experience my unhappy days, it does feel as though this isn't going to pass. However, I now realize that my mind was lying to me and trying to trick me. My thoughts and emotions were in charge of me.

Are you tired of not being happy and feeling worried, anxious, frustrated, angry, sad, or depressed? Then your thoughts and feelings are working against you. Do something about it, and take action. You have the ability to be in charge of your thoughts and emotions. Make the choice to be a happy person and live a happy life. You can find inner peace. If you can change the things that happen that you do not like, then do it.

If you can't change the things that happen that you don't like, then just let it be, and move forward. Do not stress over things that you can't control. Everything happens for a reason. Change your thinking, attitude, and perspective for the better. Are you ready for the challenge? Rise up, make it happen, and take action. You've got this—you can do it.

Step 3: Happiness is a state of mind
Remember happiness comes from within. Happiness is a choice. We need to change our negative attitudes to positive attitudes. Our mind is extraordinarily powerful. Think good, feel good. Think bad, feel bad. Happiness is a state of mind. And yes, we can create our state of mind. So, if we can create our state of mind, then we can create our happiness. Perhaps it's in your best interest to get into a whole new state of mind.

Our state of mind is our mood or mental state at a particular time. What's going on in your mind is caused by your thoughts and emotions. How do you react to: people, situations, your environment, the world? Do you have a positive state of mind or a negative state of mind? It's important to honestly reflect on and assess the current state of mind that you are in. Acknowledge it; then, if necessary, choose to change it. Our state of mind will determine our perspective on life and on the world. When your state of mind is negative, it's important to learn how to change it.

Don't be a prisoner in your own mind and be at the mercy of your thoughts and emotions. Be in charge of your mind. You are the boss of your mind. Don't let your mind be the boss of you. Create a positive-coping-skills list for yourself, and use it when you are in a negative state of mind. Get into routines that will allow you to be in a positive state of mind as much as possible. Also, don't forget to have a positive support system in place. Currently, what type of state of mind are you in? Positive state of mind or a negative state of mind?

Step 4: Gratitude is the key to happiness

We should be focusing on and appreciating what we have in our life. Start feeling grateful for what you have, and stop focusing on what you don't have. Unfortunately, we have a tendency to take things for granted. Lose your sense of entitlement. Not everybody has their health, family, friends, a roof over their head, the luxury of running water and electricity, food and beverages, shoes, clothes, a vehicle for travel, the ability to use all five senses, the capability to walk, the full use of their arms and legs, and, most importantly, a relationship with God. If you have any or all of those things, consider yourself blessed, and count your blessings. Gratitude is powerful and essential for happiness. Being ungrateful is a key ingredient in the recipe for unhappiness.

A couple of ways I choose to practice gratitude every day is through prayer and compliments. Find ways to be grateful every day, and choose to practice gratitude. You may want to consider daily routines to help you practice gratitude. I recommend creating a "Gratitude List" and writing down all the things you are thankful and grateful for. On a piece of paper, write "I am thankful for . . ." Be as specific as possible. Next to each thing you are thankful for, write the reasons why you are grateful. Read your gratitude list often—at least daily. And when you start feeling happier, keep on using your gratitude list. You will reap the benefits and begin feeling happier and more content. You can choose to be grateful or not to be grateful for what you have in your life. Gratitude = Happiness. Ungratefulness = Unhappiness.

Please don't take things for granted. Appreciate and be grateful for everything you have in your life. Develop an attitude of gratitude, and start practicing thankfulness now. Gratitude is strongly and consistently associated with greater happiness.

Step 5: Happiness is in the present moment
The only thing that exists is the present moment. The only thing that there is, ever was, or ever will be is the present moment. When you think about the "past," you are doing it in the present moment. Furthermore, if you think about a memory in the present moment, make it a positive one. There's no such thing as the "past."

When you think about the "future," you are doing it in the present moment. Don't think, *What if this happens?* or *What if that happens?* Instead, take a slow, deep, focused breath and enjoy the present moment. A lot of the things we choose to worry about don't even happen anyway. There's no such thing as "the future," because it's not here yet. Only the present moment is here—nothing else. You see, the *only* thing that exists is the present moment. Therefore, be happy for this moment, because this moment is your life. The "past" is done, the "future" is not here yet, and only the *present moment*, the *now*, exists.

I can't emphasize enough the importance of living in the present if you want to live a happy life. If you choose to start living in the present, you will begin to feel happier. Don't worry about the "future," because you're worrying about something that doesn't even exist. Don't dwell in the "past," because you will be unable to enjoy the present moment. "Past" and "future" will cause your mind to wander and jump around (monkey mind), and you will be somewhere else, not in the present. And your mind will produce brain farts. You will not feel at peace if you choose to let your mind control you like this. Your memory and your imagination will cause you suffering. When you start living in the present you can manage to control your mind, allowing you to

HAPPY: TO BE OR NOT TO BE? CHOOSE INTELLIGENTLY

feel calm, alive, and happy. And when you learn to control your mind, you can control your life. If you pay careful attention, most of your thoughts are directed mainly to the "past" or to the "future," preventing you from fully living in the present. Every thought you have produces a physical response in your nervous system and an emotional feeling in your body. Yet, we often allow our minds to go wherever it wants to go, without taking control over the direction it goes. You see, your mind wants to be your boss and in control. It wants to create chaos. To stop it, you need to stop listening to the constant chaos in your mind, stop listening to the brain farts. Be the boss of your mind, and start controlling and mastering it. Be the master of your mind. Don't let your mind be your master and make you its servant. You must be in charge of your mind—don't let your mind be in charge of you. The mind can trick us if we are not aware that it is controlling us.

So, when you become aware of your mind, you are not identified with your mind anymore. A new dimension of awareness has come in. The madness is caused by thinking without awareness, and thinking without awareness is how the ego keeps us in its grip. Cease the constant, busy activity of the mind, which is often useless, repetitive, and negative. Instead of constantly thinking, be present (be still, be silent) and stop those brain farts. Sense the aliveness within you. This is the realization of I AM, the realization of *Being*, our essence and identity. When we are rooted in that, thinking becomes the servant of awareness, rather than an ego-serving activity. Be aware of your thoughts, and don't let your ego control them and run the show. Use your brain farts as an opportunity to bring your mind back to the present moment. Don't believe those brain farts; don't believe and follow those negative thoughts, which are constantly lying to you and trying to pull you in and convince you. Laugh at the brain farts.

The quickest and most effective technique for living in the present moment is deep breathing. Take slow, deep, focused breaths. Concentrate on the sound of your breath.

One technique I use is: I inhale through my nose slowly while counting to 3. Then, I hold my breath for 1 to 3 seconds. Finally, I exhale through my mouth for as long as I can. Make sure when you breathe in through your nose, your stomach goes out, and when you breathe out through your mouth, your stomach goes back in. Practice deep breathing every day, as often as possible. It will help you to relax and live in the present moment. There are many ways to do deep breathing; find the way that works best for you.

Deep breathing will also allow you to practice mindfulness. According to the dictionary, mindfulness is a "mental state achieved by focusing one's awareness on the present moment while calmly acknowledging and accepting one's thoughts, feelings, and bodily sensations." One way I practice mindfulness is being aware of my thoughts (especially my brain farts) and how I react to them. This method of mindfulness can be helpful when you find yourself overthinking and overanalyzing situations. I now realize that at certain times in my life, like when I got married, I was overthinking, overanalyzing, and worrying excessively. That was definitely useless and not good for my well-being. It was self-defeating. I caused myself a great deal of anxiety.

Keep in mind that true happiness comes from within. The key to your peace and happiness is within you. We have a choice: We can live in the present and feel peaceful and happy and in control of our mind, or we can let our mind control our life, causing us to feel unpeaceful and unhappy. We need to work on our happiness level every day. It's all about managing our thoughts and emotions, and being in charge of them.

Step 6: Happiness Triggers—How to Create Happiness

What brings about and creates our happiness? Some may believe the answer is materialistic items. Materialistic items will never bring us true happiness. These items, no matter what we buy or keep buying, will not provide us with true happiness. Perhaps materialistic items may allow us to be temporarily happy. However, materialistic items aren't the finer things in life and will never bring us true, long-lasting happiness. The best and most extraordinary things in life are simple and free:

* Spiritual growth, a relationship with God
* Praying

HAPPY: TO BE OR NOT TO BE? CHOOSE INTELLIGENTLY

- Love
- Laughter
- Hugs
- Smiles
- Slow, deep, focused breathing
- Family
- Friends
- Appreciating what you have
- Being positive
- Helping others and situations
- Sleeping
- Expressing yourself appropriately
- The sunrise
- The sunset
- The sky
- Clouds
- The moon
- The stars
- The ocean and the sound of the waves
- Birds flying
- Birds singing
- Flowers
- Grass
- Trees

Focusing on and appreciating the beauty of nature is therapeutic and will allow us to be aware of our surroundings and live in the present moment. Nature is God's way of speaking to us and showing us his love, power, and presence. Connect with God through nature, and you will have one of the best experiences of your life.

Unfortunately, too many people are focused on and controlled by their thoughts, which usually are directed to the "past" or the "future," and they aren't living in the present. As a result, many people aren't aware of their surroundings. Losing yourself in thought is a trap of the mind. People who feel trapped in their mind are listening and believing the brain farts. Don't be a prisoner to your own thoughts; instead, live in the present, and experience being and awareness. You are not your thoughts, therefore, don't buy into them. Everyone's mind wanders; refocus your attention on the present moment. I've spent too many days of my life allowing my thoughts and emotions to be in charge of me.

Choose to be positive! Keep a positive perspective. Pray, smile, laugh, sing, and dance as much as possible. Use your positive lens. See the glass as half-full, not as half-empty. Create a positive mindset for yourself. Everything starts with our thoughts, which create our emotions. Our thoughts and choices ultimately define and shape our life.

Let love be a part of your life—the more, the merrier. Love can be from God, yourself, a partner, family, friends, pets (it's definitely not a coincidence that GOD spelled backwards is DOG), jobs, hobbies, or a neighbor. God should always come first and foremost, above all else. Love is super-powerful and a necessity in our life for true happiness. However, the first step is to love everything about ourselves. Part of being truly happy is feeling good about who you are. When you love yourself, it's easier to love someone else. A life filled with a lot of love will be a much happier life. When love is lacking, it's more likely that you will be unhappy.

Surround yourself with positive people. Positive energy is contagious. Unfortunately, so is negative energy. Therefore, surround yourself only with positive energy. If you choose to surround yourself with positive people, then chances are you'll be a positive person. Spend time with people who make you laugh and feel special and good. Spend time with people who love, appreciate, and respect you. Stay away from the negative energy and negative people.

Step 7: Understand the Reasons Why We Are Unhappy

Do you realize and understand the real reasons why you are unhappy? Probably not. List on a piece of paper all the reasons you think you are unhappy. Next to each reason, write why this makes you feel unhappy. After

HAPPY: TO BE OR NOT TO BE? CHOOSE INTELLIGENTLY

that, reflect upon and question the reasons. Quite often, our reasons and our beliefs are irrational. Don't blame others; you are responsible and accountable for what you say and do.

Furthermore, forget about what other people think. When others express their opinions, look at who it's coming from, and many times you will see that their opinion really doesn't matter. Why do you listen to the negative opinions of others? Choose not to listen to these opinions. I don't listen to most opinions. God's opinion matters, your opinion of yourself matters, and the opinion of certain family members and friends matters. That's it! Everybody has an opinion. And those opinions have a tendency to stink and be negative. Don't let the opinions of others influence, damage, or affect you. Their opinion of you is their problem, not yours. Don't make the opinions of others your problem or change who you are. Opinions of others are not facts, they are just opinions. Keep your inner light shining bright. You determine your own self-worth and self-concept. They are not created or found in the opinions of others. In life you will meet two kinds of people. Ones who build you up, and ones who tear you down. But in the end, you will thank them both.

Don't compare yourself to others or situations. Don't worry about keeping up with the Joneses. When materialism becomes a priority, your happiness level will decline. Don't attach your sense of worth to material items or to what others think of you. If you choose to do this, you will never experience long-lasting, true happiness. Failure results when you start comparing yourself with others. (2)

The egoic mind doesn't know your true self, lives in the "past" and "future," loves the 3 Cs—Complaining, Critcizing, and Comparing—blames others, doesn't accept responsibility or accountability for words and actions, is often bothered by what other people think and their opinions, often compares yourself to others and situations, wants more and more and more in order to keep up with the Joneses, and is never satisfied or happy.

The free mind knows your true self, lives in the present moment, is calm, secure, and complimentary, accepts responsibility and accountability for words and actions, is not affected by other people's thoughts and opinions, doesn't compare yourself to others or situations, doesn't want more and more and more, isn't concerned about keeping up with the Joneses, and is satisfied and happy.

The egoic mind is never content but insecure and doesn't appreciate things you have in your life. The free mind is content, secure, and appreciates everything that you have in your life. Utilize your free mind to see your true self, which is Being, Awareness, spirit, soul, and bliss.

Ultimately, you are the only person who can cause your unhappiness. You can choose to be your own best friend and let the free mind do the thinking, or you can choose to be your own worst enemy and let the egoic mind do the thinking. Free mind = you are in charge of your thoughts and emotions. Egoic mind = your thoughts and emotions are in charge of you. The choice is yours and only yours.

Eckhart Tolle said, "The decision to make the present moment into your friend is the end of ego." Let go of thought, become still and alert, and don't allow your thoughts and feelings to control you. When you are present, you can allow the mind to be as it is, without getting entangled in it. The mind itself is a wonderful tool. Dysfunction sets in when you seek yourself in it and mistake it for who you are. How strongly are you identified with your mind?

According to Tolle, why does the mind habitually deny or resist the *Now*? Because it cannot function and remain in control without time, which is past and future, so it perceives the timeless *Now* as threatening. Time and mind are, in fact, inseparable.

Be present as the watcher of your mind—of your thoughts and emotions, as well as your reactions, in various situations. Be at least as interested in your reactions as in the person or situation that causes you to react.

How do you practice happiness? Pay attention to your automatic emotional reactions. You want to begin consciously challenging the negative thoughts and limiting belief systems that underlie them. Remember, you are not your thoughts. You are Being, Awareness, I AM.

After God, the most important relationship you will have is with yourself, especially your relationship with the present moment. Silence or ignore the voice

HAPPY: TO BE OR NOT TO BE? CHOOSE INTELLIGENTLY

in your head. Focus and concentrate your attention on the present moment. Happiness comes from where we give our attention to. Keep directing yourself to the present moment. Stay grounded, present, and in the moment—be still, be silent. A crucial relationship in your life is your relationship with the present moment. Are you in touch and at peace with the present moment? What do you do to stay in touch and at peace with the present moment? For me, I pray, do slow, deep, focused breathing, or look at nature.

Once you have reached a certain level of awareness of something within yourself that's not conditioned, then you are able to decide what kind of relationship you want to have with the present moment. The present moment and life can't be separated, so you are really deciding what kind of a relationship you want to have with life.

Our natural state of Being is joy. You *are* Being, therefore, be—*just be*. Don't be this, or don't be that. Accept every moment as it is. In whatever you do, your state of awareness is of utmost importance. Let the sense of I AM come to the forefront of your present-moment experience. Not I AM this or I AM that—just I AM. Let your attention be focused on your Being. Your Being is always unchanging in the here and now. Sense your Awareness and Being in the present moment. Know and feel that you exist in the present moment. You exist in this very moment. *Just see, just be.*

Experience Awareness and Being by living in the present moment, and this calm, happy, relaxing feeling will arise from within you. Being must be felt. It can't be thought. True happiness lies within us if we can just be, be still, be silent. Let your being emerge, and feel the aliveness within you. It takes a certain amount of practice and training to be able to be still, to be silent, and reach a high level of Awareness.

Our thoughts demand our attention. Don't give the thoughts the attention they want. Free yourself from damaging thoughts, and don't let negative emotions control you, especially anger and hate. This is what the egoic mind wants to do. Happiness depends upon your ability to manage your thoughts and emotions. Make your mind work for you, not against you. Do you identify, attach, and react to your thoughts and emotions? My mind is constantly trying to take me to "past" and "future"—and continually producing unpleasant thoughts. Quite often throughout the day, I have to take a slow, deep, focused breath to take my mind back to the present moment. How we deal with and respond to our thoughts and emotions means everything. What do you do when your mind is jumping around all over the place and producing brain farts?

Don't think too much—it causes too many problems for you, including overthinking, overanalyzing, overcomplicating, and overreacting. When you think too long, you might think wrong. Keep life simple; don't complicate it.

Thinking without awareness is the main dilemma of human existence. Be aware of your thinking and what it is trying to do to you; stick with the facts. The more you identify with your thoughts, emotions, reactions, and beliefs, the less Being you experience. When you identify with something, you make it the same—the same as *I*. It becomes part of your identity. Thoughts change and come and go like the clouds, but the sense that you exist always remains, like the sky. You are not your thoughts; you are not your feelings. You are Being, just like the sky.

Most people are so distracted by their thoughts, so identified with the voices in their heads, they can no longer feel the aliveness within them, the very life that you are (Being, Awareness, spirit, soul, and bliss). They hardly enjoy the present moment because they are in the grip of the egoic mind. *Pleeease* don't deprive yourself of enjoying the present moment. It's the only thing we have.

With awareness comes dis-identification from thoughts, emotions, reactions, and beliefs. Before you were the thoughts, emotions, reactions, and beliefs; now you are the Awareness and Being that witnesses those states. All you need to do is be aware of your thoughts and emotions, as they happen. Be alert and observe. Thoughts and emotions become depersonalized through Awareness. Let go of identification with your mind. Who you are beyond the mind then emerges by itself.

But not if the ego has anything to say about it. To be in the grip of the ego is to be completely identified with your mind and its constant stream of thoughts. Ego implies unawareness. Ego is identifying with your thoughts and

HAPPY: TO BE OR NOT TO BE? CHOOSE INTELLIGENTLY

feelings. Ego is a dysfunctional relationship with the present moment. Ego lives through comparison (I vs. other). Under your physical and psychological form, you are being. In form, you will always be inferior to some, superior to others. Truthfully, you are neither inferior nor superior to anyone. The truth shall set you free. Do not take the ego too seriously. When you detect egoic behavior in yourself, smile and laugh. To become free of the ego is to be aware of it, since Awareness and ego can't exist together. The decision to make the present moment into your friend is the end of the ego. Be aware of your Being. I AM.

The ego tends to equate *having* with Being: I have, therefore I am. And the more I have, the more I am. Trying to find yourself through things doesn't work—you will get lost. The satisfaction of the ego is short-lived, and so you want more. Nothing can satisfy the ego for long, hence greed and selfishness. Don't let the ego run or ruin your life.

Time—that is to say, past and future—is what the false mind-made self, the ego, lives on. The stronger the ego, the more time takes over your life. Almost every thought you think is then concerned with past or future, and your sense of self depends on the past for your identity and on the future for its fulfillment. This is exactly how my anxiety was triggered after I got married. Relentlessly, my mind kept taking me back to my parents' divorce. And my mind kept repeatedly trying to convince me that I was going to end up divorced just like my parents, and why did I even bother to get married. I was buying in to these brain farts on and off for a few years. I fell into a trap set by my mind. I was in the grip of my egoic mind. Slow down your mind, and don't think too much. Don't let your thoughts constantly bring you to the "past" and "future"—especially since "past" and "future" don't exist. Do not let your thoughts constantly have your attention. Concentrate and focus your attention on the present moment. Everything happens in the present moment. The present moment is all we have. The elimination of time (meaning "past" and "future") from your being is the elimination of ego. This is a powerful spiritual practice.

We all desire and need to have a sense of accomplishment, which will contribute to our overall level of happiness. We all want to accomplish something worthwhile. Find the meaning in your life. We all need meaning in life. What gives me the most meaning in my life are the following roles: God's Child, a father, a husband, a family member, a school counselor, a dog dad, and a friend. These roles also provide me with value and happiness. I believe these roles have created value in my life and the lives of others. Be the best at whatever it is that you value. In all your roles, show you care, and do your best.

One important way to be happy is to dedicate some time during the day to yourself, to do something that you really like. It could be anything, but it must be your time. Something that creates balance and lightness in your life. Create *me* time every day for yourself, even if it's for 10 minutes a day—get it done. Self-care has to be and remain a top priority in your life.

How to Create a Self-Care Plan for Yourself

Step 1. Learn about the importance of self-care.
Self-care is an important part of staying happy and healthy. Have a strategy or plan that will help you deal with issues in your life, especially managing your stress level and everyday stressors. Self-care is very important for dealing with and managing stress. Make it a priority to take care of yourself.

Step 2. Determine your stress level.
It's important for you to recognize the level of stress in your life and how it is affecting you.

Rate your stress level on a scale of 1 to 10.

* 1 to 3 Not Stressed
* 4 to 6 A Little Stressed
* 7 & 8 Stressed
* 9 & 10 Very Stressed

HAPPY: TO BE OR NOT TO BE? CHOOSE INTELLIGENTLY

Step 3. Identify stressors
Reflect on and make a list of what causes you stress in your life.

Step 4. Recognize how you typically cope with stress.
List your current coping strategies.

Step 5. Create a personalized self-care plan for yourself.
I find that prayer, deep breathing, and exercise work well for me.

Step 6. Utilizing your self-care plan.
How are you going to put your plan into action? How will you hold yourself accountable for implementing your self-care plan? Make a commitment to it. Share your plan with family and friends.

Step 7. Evaluating the self-care plan
What is working? What is not working? Adjust the plan accordingly.

For self-care to work, it involves:

1. Deciding that self-care is important
2. Creating a plan (Finding what works)
3. Committing to the self-care plan
4. Evaluating the plan (Changes, adjustments)

Having a self-care plan for yourself is essential. How are you taking great care of yourself? What is your self-care plan? July 24th is International Self-Care Day. This special day is an opportunity to spotlight the value of self-care practices, and the approaches people use every day to maximize their physical and mental health.

Feeling better starts with you. Please create and maintain a self-care plan that works well for you. Strive to make self-care a priority every day.

CHOOSING TRUE HAPPINESS

Depression is an illness, not a weakness. Find helpful ways to manage your emotions, especially sadness, depression, and anger. Constantly express your feelings in an appropriate manner. Don't hold in your feelings. This is what I did after my parents divorce. Please learn from my mistake. Holding in your feelings is a harmful way to manage your emotions. And is a recipe for disaster. Let go of disgust, frustration, anger, sadness, depression, guilt, and any other negative emotions. Think of positive memories. And only visit things that happen to learn from your mistakes or for a beautiful memory. Mismanaging your thoughts and memories causes sadness, depression, and anger. Remember only the present moment exists, there's no such thing as "past". Train your brain and redirect your thoughts and awareness back to the present moment. Try to stay in the moment as much as possible.

Anxiety is your imagination gone haywire. Don't let your imagination go out of control and be erratic. This is what I did for the first few years after I got married. Please learn from my mistake. Mismanaging your thoughts and imagination causes worry and anxiety. Only visit things that could happen for planning and/or setting goals. Remember only the present moment exists, there's no such thing as future. Give attention to the now frequently.

You cannot suffer from the past or future because they do not exist. What you are suffering from is the misuse of your memory and your imagination. If you know how to handle your thoughts and emotions, there will be no such thing as depression or anxiety for you.

We all want to be happy. We search for happiness throughout our lifetime. However, the peace, happiness, joy, and bliss we have been searching for, even competing for, have been here all along in our Awareness and Being. We are that peace, happiness, joy, and bliss. Concentrate, focus on, and bring your attention to the present moment. Experience it as much as possible. Be aware of, enjoy, and live in the present moment. Say "Yes" to the present moment, and make it into your friend. Welcome to the present moment, the *here and now*—the only moment there ever is. We already are what we spend our lives trying to attain. We fulfill our destiny and realize our purpose when we awaken to who we truly are: Awareness, Being, spirit, soul, and bliss.

HAPPY: TO BE OR NOT TO BE? CHOOSE INTELLIGENTLY

Realize who you truly are and that true happiness comes from within. Feel the power of the present moment and the fullness of your being. *Be, just be.* May you experience the most profound moments of stillness and insight of the within (Awareness, Being, spirit, soul, and bliss). Let your thinking and mind work for you, not against you. Being in charge of your thoughts and emotions is definitely challenging and by no means an easy task. You have the ability to manage your thoughts and emotions. It requires practice, focus and awareness. However, I believe in you! You've got this—you can do this! Choose to be happy, and lead a life filled with peace and joy.

If you want to be truly happy, you'll need to work at it. There are no shortcuts to happiness and success. The things that will make us happiest and successful require effort. Avoid things that bring instant gratification and short-lived happiness. Slow and steady win's the race. Choose to do things that bring you lasting, true happiness and live a fulfilling life. When I was around 38 years old, I started examining and changing my self-destructive mental, emotional and behavioral patterns. And I realized that it all started with my negative thinking, holding in my feelings, and not reaching out for help. I was able to change my thinking, express myself appropriately, and make better choices. This allowed me to reap the rewards of true and lasting happiness for the past twelve years. If I was able to do it, then you can definitely do it!

We all have a moral obligation to ourselves and one another to make this world a better place. Let's all do the right thing for ourselves and others.

When it's all said and done, I believe there are three questions that we should have great answers for:

1. Who did you help?
2. What did you learn?
3. What did you accomplish?

The answers for all three of these questions should involve having a positive impact on the lives of others and situations. At the end of this lifetime, the only things that will matter are:

CHOOSING TRUE HAPPINESS

How did your life impact the lives of others and situations? How did you make this world a better place?

How does your life impact the lives of others and situations?

How are you making this world a better place?

What legacy will you leave behind?

Throughout the book, I've shared some of my favorite quotes with you. I wanted to provide you with these quotes in the hope that they: give you knowledge, motivation, a guideline of words to live by, influence you, and impact your life in a positive way. And help you be more peaceful and happier. Lastly, I hope you love these quotes as much as I do.

Words of Wisdom
Words of Inspiration
Words to Live By

"Some people come in your life as blessings. Some come in your life as lessons."
—MOTHER TERESA (3)

"Everyone is going through something."
—KEVIN LOVE (4)

"You must expect great things of yourself before you can do them."
—MICHAEL JORDAN (5)

"None of us should assume stuff."
—ADAM VINATIERI (6)

HAPPY: TO BE OR NOT TO BE? CHOOSE INTELLIGENTLY

"Believe in your dreams. Believe in today. Believe that you are loved. Believe that you make a difference. Believe we can build a better world. Believe when others might not. Believe there's a light at the end of the tunnel. Believe that you might be that light for someone else. Believe that the best is yet to be. Believe in each other. Believe in yourself. I believe in you."
—Kobi Yamada (7)

"The starting place for your greatness is desire. The desire to succeed, to serve others, to keep on going no matter what; the desire to . . ."
—Assegid Habtewold (8)

"Peace is not something you wish for: It's something you make, something you do, something you are, and something you give away."
—John Lennon (9)

"There can be no peace without justice, no justice without law and no meaningful law without a Court to decide what is just and lawful under any given circumstance."
—Benjamin B. Ferencz (10)

"Once you shift your order of priorities from 'having-doing-being' to 'being-doing-having,' your destiny will be in your hands."
—Sadhguru (11)

"The greatest weapon against stress is our ability to choose one thought over another."
—William James (12)

CHOOSING TRUE HAPPINESS

"I'm no stranger to pain. It's what made me."
—DeMar DeRozan (13)

"Happiness is when what you think, what you say, and what you do are in harmony."
—Mahatma Gandhi (14)

"I believe that all people that are successful should pay back their cities, their states, their towns, our country."
—John Catsimatidis (15)

"A person's most useful asset is not a head full of knowledge, but a heart full of love, an ear ready to listen, and a hand willing to help."
—Unknown (16)

"I always have tried to treat people with respect, the way I want to be treated."
—Derek Jeter (17)

"God is everywhere and in everything and without Him we cannot exist."
—Mother Teresa (18)

"I'm a weird big guy. Doing rapping, doing movies. Do a lot of stuff. But always do things the right way."
—Shaquille O'Neal (19)

HAPPY: TO BE OR NOT TO BE? CHOOSE INTELLIGENTLY

The Greatest Man in History . . . Jesus; Had no servants, yet they called Him Master. Had no degree, yet they called Him Teacher. Had no medicines, yet they called Him Healer. He had no army, yet kings feared Him. He won no military battles, yet He conquered the world. He did not live in a castle, yet they called Him Lord. He ruled no nations, yet they called Him King. He committed no crime, yet they crucified Him. He was buried in a tomb, yet He lives today.
—Lyle C. Rollings III, 2008 (20)

"Life is an opportunity, benefit from it. Life is beauty, admire it. Life is a dream, realize it. Life is a challenge, meet it. Life is a duty, complete it. Life is a game, play it. Life is a promise, fulfill it. Life is sorrow, overcome it. Life is a song, sing it. Life is a struggle, accept it. Life is a tragedy, confront it. Life is an adventure, dare it. Life is luck, make it. Life is too precious, do not destroy it. Life is life, fight for it."
—Mother Teresa (21)

You have to change your life if you're not happy, and wake up if things aren't going the way you want.
—Keanu Reeves (22)

"Stand in the face of adversity. Stand for an idea. Stand to empower the world."
—Chris Norton (23)

"Just do the best with what you have, and you'll soon be doing it better."
—Gil Hodges (24)

CHOOSING TRUE HAPPINESS

"If you're willing to put yourself and your dreams on the line, at the very least you'll discover an inner strength you may not have known existed."
—Kurt Warner (25)

"I'm not perfect; no one is perfect. Everyone makes mistakes. I think you try to learn from those mistakes."
—Derek Jeter (26)

"One is only happy in proportion as he makes others feel happy and only useful as he contributes his influences for the finer callings in life."
—Milton S. Hershey (27)

"Your happiness is your own responsibility."
—Jennifer Garner (28)

"Though no one can go back and make a brand new start, anyone can start from now and make a brand new ending."
—Carl Bard (29)

"Don't give up. Don't ever give up."
—Jim Valvano (30)

Reflect and think about the quotes in this book. Which quotes resonated with you best?

CHAPTER TWENTY
The Most and the Greatest

The greatest joy . . . . Giving

The most useless thing to do . . . . Worry

The most beautiful attire. . . . . Smile

The greatest loss . . . . Loss of Self-Respect

The two most powerful words . . . . I Can

The greatest problem to overcome . . . . Fear

The greatest computer . . . . The Brain

The most crippling disease . . . . Excuses

The ugliest trait . . . . Selfishness

The greatest sleeping pill . . . . Peace

The worst thing to be without . . . . Hope

CHOOSING TRUE HAPPINESS

The most dangerous pariah . . . . A Gossiper

The deadliest weapon . . . . The Tongue

The most powerful communication . . . . Prayer

The most satisfying work . . . . Helping Others

The greatest asset . . . . Faith

The most worthless emotion . . . . Self-Pity

The most contagious spirit . . . . Enthusiasm

The most prized possession . . . . Integrity

The greatest shot in the arm . . . . . . Encouragement

The most powerful force . . . . Love

The most important thing in life . . . . God
—C<small>ARL</small> P<small>ALMIERI</small>

CHAPTER TWENTY-ONE
Daily Happiness Checklist

* It all starts and ends with you
* Pray
* Seek and connect with God
* Do one thing to improve your relationship with God and yourself
* Slow, deep, focused breathing (2 to 15 minutes)
* Say positive affirmations (I am strong, I am relaxed)
* Manage your thoughts and emotions
* Hug family members, friends, and pets (heart to heart, at least 20 seconds)
* Laugh
* Stay positive with your thoughts, words, and actions
* Admire nature
* Drink a lot of water
* Use your sense of humor as much as possible
* Focus on and show appreciation (All aspects of your life—concentrate on what you have)
* Exercise
* Count three of your blessings (Think about them, and say them or write them down)
* Eat a healthy diet
* Compliment and respect someone

CHOOSING TRUE HAPPINESS

- Tell and show somebody you love them
- Do one kind deed (help someone)
- Write in a journal or on any piece of paper (express your thoughts and feelings)
- Do one thing to improve a relationship
- Start or maintain a positive support system
- Work toward your goal and dreams
- Get a good night's sleep (7 to 9 hours)
- Do your best each and every day; strive to be your best self every day
- Be focused, determined, and persistent when following this checklist

If you choose to follow this daily happiness checklist, you will reap the benefits. Make the intelligent, responsible choice to follow this check list on a daily basis. You decide. Choose intelligently.

CHAPTER TWENTY-TWO
ABCs of Happiness

Appreciating and Accepting
Believing
Choices, Compassion and Courage
Dedicated and Determined
Empathetic
Faithful (Faith is believing and feeling the unseen)
God first above all else
Helpful, Hopeful and Honest
I, it all starts and ends with you
Joke a lot
Kindness counts
Love, Love, Love (Spread it everywhere)
Make a self-care plan
Nutrition (Keep it healthy)
Only observe and don't identify or become engaged with your thoughts, feelings, or opinions that are not beneficial for you
Pray, Patience, and Present (Live in the present moment)
Quietly be
Relationships, make them loving and fulfilling
Sleep well and Smile a lot
Take charge of your mind (Keep a positive mindset)

CHOOSING TRUE HAPPINESS

Understanding
Viewpoint (Positive Perspective)
Wisdom (Learn from Experiences)
Xercise
Yearn for Happiness
Zest for life

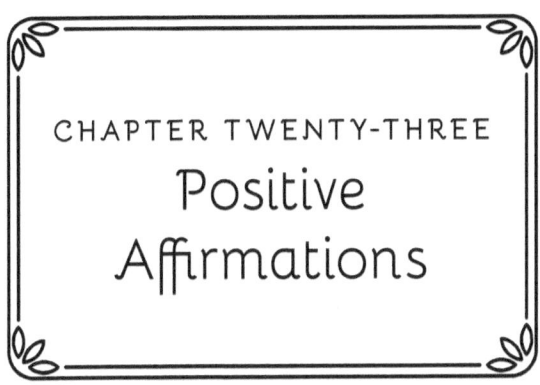

CHAPTER TWENTY-THREE
Positive Affirmations

Positive affirmations are statements that are repeated to uplift, encourage, and give confidence, peace, and happiness to the person speaking them.

Your brain responds best to present-tense affirmations. Everything that happens is happening in the moment for your brain. Your brain is eager to set you up for success—all you have to do is instruct it. Set up a routine that works for you, like repeating the affirmation 25 times, 3 times a day. The key to a successful affirmation is belief. Whatever the mind of a person can perceive and believe, it can achieve. Positive affirmations are powerful tools for making your life better.

Positive affirmations will help reprogram our subconscious to think positively. Our minds are like computers that can be programmed. We choose the software to be beneficial or non-beneficial. Our mind believes what we tell it.

Affirmations repeated several times each day, every day, serve to reprogram your subconscious with positive thinking.

An affirmation is made up of words charged with power, conviction, and faith. You send a positive response to your subconscious, which accepts whatever you tell it. When done properly, this triggers positive feelings that, in turn, get results and drive action.

Here are some examples of positive affirmations:

CHOOSING TRUE HAPPINESS

- I thank, serve, and love God every day
- Centered in God, I am secure and peaceful
- I believe in the power of prayer
- I believe in the power of faith
- I believe in the power of love
- I welcome every blessing in a spirit of gratitude and generosity
- My eyes can see the beautiful potential within and all around me
- I am with God, and God is with me always
- I am responsible for my spiritual growth
- I choose to be happy
- I am present in every moment
- I am enough
- I count my blessings daily
- I am being
- I am existence
- I am strong
- I am calm
- I am relaxed
- I am thankful for my health (walking, seeing, hearing, and talking)
- I choose to be positive
- I think positively and find the positive in everything
- I focus on the positive
- I have a positive perspective
- I always see the bright side in life
- I choose to see only the positive
- I get to choose positive responses
- I choose how I feel
- I focus on what I have
- I strive for what I want
- I remain positive, hopeful, and productive
- I have good relationships in my life
- I appreciate all the things I have in my life

POSITIVE AFFIRMATIONS

- I show appreciation to others
- I choose to sing and dance
- I am open to laughter every day
- I use my sense of humor quite often
- I find humor in things and laugh every day
- I am helpful to a lot of people
- I choose exercise
- I really enjoy the energy that exercise gives me
- I choose love
- I am open to give and receive love
- I choose peace
- I love myself and, in turn, attract love
- Hugging provides healing
- I do express myself in a positive way
- I alone control my attitude
- I am responsible for my own beliefs and attitudes
- I keep a positive attitude at all times
- I set specific intentions to achieve my dream
- I know, accept, and am true to myself
- I learn from my mistakes
- I never give up
- I enjoy life to the fullest
- I accept others for who they are
- I strive to be my best self
- I am loving and lovable
- All of my relationships are positive and filled with love and compassion
- I find opportunities to be kind and caring everywhere I look
- Each day of my life is filled with happiness and love
- I desire only things that are healthy for me
- My thoughts and feelings work for me
- I see beauty everywhere
- I deserve to be happy and healthy

CHOOSING TRUE HAPPINESS

- I love myself enough to take better care of myself
- I am learning and growing every day
- I know my happiness depends on me
- I control my actions and my results
- I have all the help and support I need
- I have a positive support system
- Believe! There's always hope, help, and faith!
- I am determined and persistent to conquer all things
- I have strength, courage, and willpower
- I have mental toughness
- I vow to live one day at a time
- I stay present in the moment
- I am fully focused and present in my interactions
- I choose to move forward
- I move forward fearlessly and excitedly
- I choose to eat healthy
- I do know sleep is the best meditation
- I now enter a place of deep and restful sleep
- The only person I want to be is a better version of myself
- I am determined to be who I am really meant to be
- I have the will to win
- I know everything is an opportunity
- I have a growth mindset
- I am a warrior
- I know this, too, shall pass
- I am committing myself to live a happy life
- I choose to create a happy life
- I am happy
- I can be my best self and live my best life
- Write your own positive affirmations

CHAPTER TWENTY-FOUR
In a Nutshell

- Seek and connect with God
- Believe, trust, and have faith in God
- Thank and love God, and grow spiritually
- Pray daily. Prayer can move mountains.
- You need to make the choice to be happy. Everything starts and ends with you and your thinking
- Manage your thoughts and emotions. Be in charge of your thoughts and emotions! You are not your thoughts. You are not your feelings.
- Live in the present moment
- Keep and build only positive, healthy, loving relationships
- Appreciate everything you have in your life (Have a thankful mindset)
- Maintain a positive perspective; there's a silver lining in everything
- Have a positive support system in place
- Eat a healthy, balanced diet
- Laugh often; use your sense of humor a lot (Don't go a day without laughing)
- Help others and situations frequently
- Exercise (No sweat, no glory)
- Be very loving, and spread the love
- Get enough quality sleep (7 to 9 hours)

CHOOSING TRUE HAPPINESS

* Hug family members, friends, and pets every day (heart to heart, at least 20 seconds)
* Express yourself
* Positive and grateful attitude toward life; make it contagious (attitude of gratitude)
* Believe, work on, and follow your dreams
* Every day, be loving, respectful, kind, and compassionate toward people and situations.
* Be your best self every day (Be the kindest/nicest person that you can be each day and make your next days your best days)

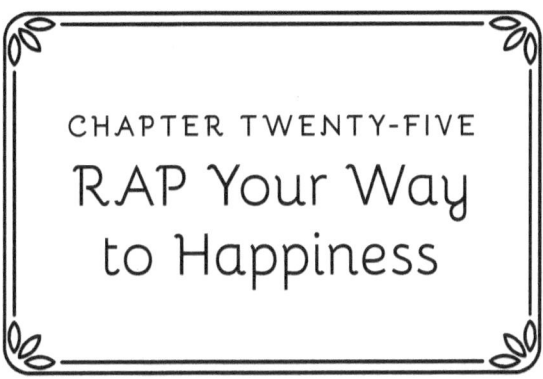

CHAPTER TWENTY-FIVE
RAP Your Way to Happiness

Relationships
Appreciation
Perspective

CHAPTER TWENTY-SIX
TEA

Thinking
Emotions
Actions

Are all connected to one another. Each one affects the other two. However, it all starts with your thinking.

* Thinking creates Emotions and Actions (What we think affects how we feel and act)
* Emotions influence your Thinking and Actions (How we feel affects what we think and do)
* Actions affect your Thinking and Emotions (What we do affects how we think and feel)

Observe and manage the TEA in your life.

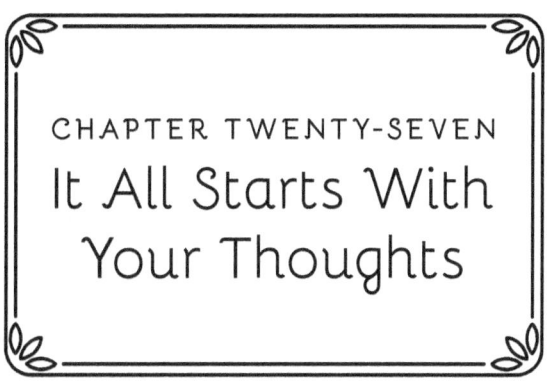

CHAPTER TWENTY-SEVEN
It All Starts With Your Thoughts

Keep it positive.
Good thoughts, Good feelings, Good words, Good actions.

How you think leads to what you say.
What you say leads to what you do.
What you do becomes your pattern.
Your patterns become who you are.
And who you are becomes your destiny.

Thoughts
↓
Words
↓
Actions
↓
Habits
↓
Character
↓
Destiny

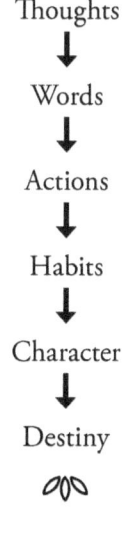

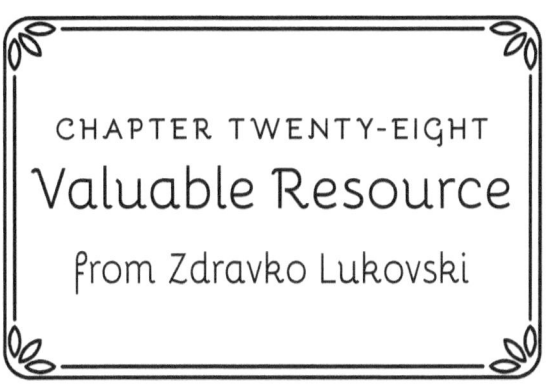

CHAPTER TWENTY-EIGHT
Valuable Resource
from Zdravko Lukovski

Pleeease visit this great website and find *aaamazing* resources. It's definitely a game changer.

> 10 Positive Thinking Exercises and Activities
> That Will Change Your Life
> 5 Bonus Tips that you should consider
> —Zdravko Lukovski
>
> *https://enlightenmentportal.com/development/positive-thinking-exercises-and-activities/*
> Thank you, Zdravko!!!

CHAPTER TWENTY-NINE
Mother Teresa's Message

The version found written on the wall in Mother Teresa's home for children in Calcutta, and it is credited to Mother Teresa:

> People are often unreasonable, irrational,
> and self-centered. Forgive them anyway.
>
> If you are kind, people may accuse you of
> selfish, ulterior motives. Be kind anyway.
>
> If you are successful, you will win some unfaithful
> friends and some genuine enemies. Succeed anyway.
>
> If you are honest and sincere, people may deceive
> you. Be honest and sincere anyway.
>
> What you spend years creating, others could
> destroy overnight. Create anyway.
>
> If you find serenity and happiness, some
> may be jealous. Be happy anyway.

CHOOSING TRUE HAPPINESS

The good you do today will often be forgotten.
Do good anyway.

Give the best you have, and it will never be enough.
Give your best anyway.

In the final analysis, it is between you and God.
It was never between you and them anyway.

I *wrote these lyrics and put them to the tune* of Ed Sheeran's song "Perfect." I love that song. Thank you, Ed!
Sing my lyrics to the tune of "Perfect"

"Jesus in Me"

I found my Jesus, in me
Just stay by His side
And follow His lead
Well, I found my Jesus, oh so sweet
I never knew He was always right by me
'Cause I was just trying to find my way

Not knowing everything He is
I will not stop following Him this time
Oh, Jesus, just show me You're there and
how much You always care
And I want You to show me my path

CHOOSING TRUE HAPPINESS

Jesus, I'm praying in the dark,
With You right by my side
Thinking of the cross, with tears coming to my eyes
When You said You are the way,
You were showing me my path, Now I know it,
Jesus You are perfect always

Well, I found my Jesus, stronger than anyone I know
He shares my dreams,
I hope that someday I share His home
I found my Jesus, Who listens to my prayers, Who shows me love, Who gives me blessings of my own

We're all God's Children, and He loves us so much
Giving His Son for us
I will be thankful right now
Oh, Jesus, I want to hold Your hand
You're my Lord, I want to be Your biggest fan
I see my future in Your home

Jesus, I'm praying in the dark,
With You right by my side
Thinking of the cross, with tears coming to my eyes
When I see You on the cross, sacrificing everything
I don't deserve this, Jesus, You are perfect always

Jesus, I'm praying in the dark,
With You right by my side
Thinking of the cross, with tears coming to my eyes
I have faith in what I can't see
Now I do believe in Jesus Christ

SPECIAL SONG

And He's Our Savior
We don't deserve Him
Jesus, You are perfect, always

CHAPTER THIRTY-ONE
What If . . .

What if everyone realized that we are all God's
Children, part of one family, God's Family

What if everyone made good choices
for themselves and others

What if people didn't negatively judge
and criticize one another and verbalized positive opinions

What if everyone was the change
they wanted to see in the world

What if all humans were treated fairly and equally,
regardless of their gender, race, or religion

What if everyone treated each other with love,
respect, kindness, and compassion

What if people, animals, and all living things
came before money

CHOOSING TRUE HAPPINESS

What if Mother Earth came before money

What if people didn't need power and
control over others and situations

What if you do your part to make
this world a better place

What if tomorrow was the beginning
of a whole new world

What if . . .

It's possible, if we all choose to do so.

It's up to us.

Each one of us has the power to change.

Each one of us has the free will to make
choices that are good for everybody.

"May all of us have the courage, commitment,
and the consciousness to make better humans
of ourselves, and, in turn, a better world."
—Sadhguru (1)

CHAPTER THIRTY-TWO
Grace

My version of saying grace before dinner:

Sign of the Cross

"Bless us, O Lord, and these, Thy gifts, which we are about to receive from Thy bounty. Through Christ, our Lord. Amen."
Thank you, God, for our many blessings.
Please keep our family happy, healthy, and safe.
Thank you, God, for always loving us and being by our side.
God, please help the sick people, poor people, and victims of tragedies.
God please help the people in Ukraine
God, please help us to have a special, strong, loving relationship with you.
Thank you for our military, who serve us, protect us, and give us our freedom.
God, please help us to follow the 2 Great Commandments, love you and others.
Sign of the Cross

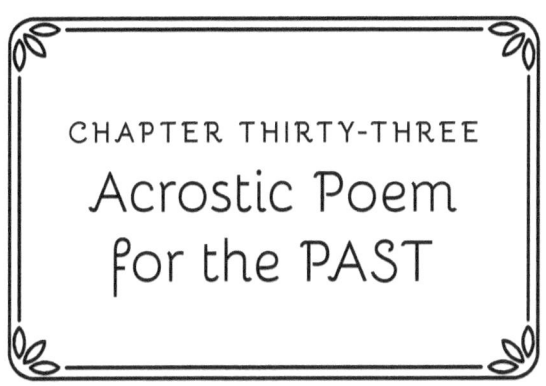

CHAPTER THIRTY-THREE
Acrostic Poem for the PAST

Positive, beautiful memories only

As you learn to accept it

Smile, let it go, and keep the lesson it taught you

To learn from a mistake or experience

> "Life is really like that: there are certain things that are wonderful and certain things that are not so wonderful and what are you going to do about it. With grace and with dignity, move through them. Deal with them."
> —Harry Connick, Jr. (1)

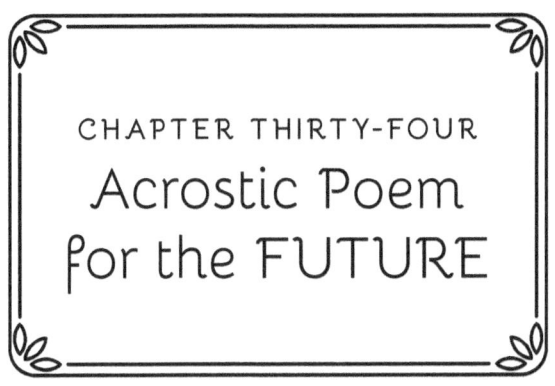

CHAPTER THIRTY-FOUR
Acrostic Poem for the FUTURE

For setting goals

Unattached to negative thoughts toward it

Take a slow, deep, focused breath; it is not yet

Use it for planning and dreaming big

Remain committed to excellence

Enable hope, positivity, and enthusiasm

> "A truly intelligent mind is neither influenced by memory nor deluded by imagination."
> —SADHGURU (1)

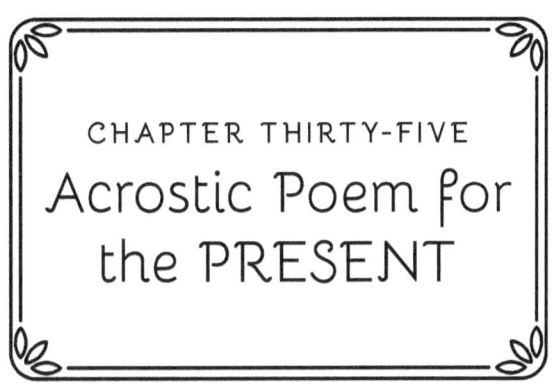

CHAPTER THIRTY-FIVE
Acrostic Poem for the PRESENT

Precious gift

Remain grounded in it

Engaged in the now

Seize the moment

Enormously thankful

Nothing but your best

The only thing that really *is*

> "Living in the moment means letting go of the past and not waiting for the future. It means living your life consciously, aware that each moment you breathe is a gift."
> —Oprah Winfrey (1)

CHAPTER THIRTY-SIX
A theme to live by for each day of the week!

Make A Difference Mondays
Thankful Tuesdays
Willpower Wednesdays
Take-Charge Thursdays
Feel-Good Fridays
Smiling Saturdays
Serene Sundays

"No matter how long your journey appears to be, there is never more than this: one step, one breath, one moment . . . Now."
—Eckhart Tolle (1)

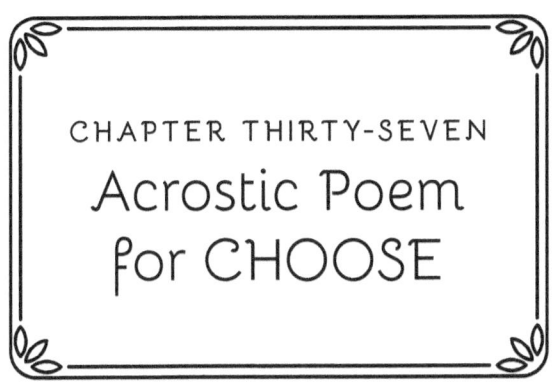

CHAPTER THIRTY-SEVEN
Acrostic Poem for CHOOSE

We are responsible for our words and actions. Think before you speak or act. There are consequences for what you say and do. Our lives are shaped by the choices that we make.

Calmly determine your choice

Happiness should be a priority

Opportunity to compare and think about the choices

Objective is happiness

Select your choice carefully; do the right thing for yourself and others

Evaluate the choice

> "Happiness is not by chance, but by choice."
> —JIM ROHN (1)

CHAPTER THIRTY-EIGHT
The 3's

How do the three's relate in your life?
How do the three's affect your thoughts, words, emotions, and actions? How are the three's connected to your happiness level and overall well-being?

The Three A's
Attitude
Appreciation
Accomplishments

The Three B's
Breathe (slow, deep, and focused)
Be yourself
Believe in yourself

The Three C's
Complaining
Criticizing
Comparing

The Three C's
Character
Courage
Committment

CHOOSING TRUE HAPPINESS

The Three D's
Decisions
Determination
Dreams

The Three D's
Desire
Dedication
Discipline
Wow! The Three D's are awesome baby!
Love you Dickie V! ♥ ♥ ♥

The Three E's
Empathy
Exercise
Express Yourself

The Three F's
Faith
Family
Forgiveness

The Three G's
Generous
Good-hearted
Good sleep

The Three H's
Healthy
Hugs
Happiness

THE 3'S

The Three H's
Honesty
Habits
Hardworking

The Three I's
I
Intelligence
Improvement

The Three I's
Insightful
Inspire
Integrity

The Three J's
Joke a lot
Just
Joyful

The Three K's
Knowledge
Kindness
Karma

The Three L's
Love (especially God and yourself)
Laugh
Learn

The Three M's
Meditate
Meaning
Moderation

CHOOSING TRUE HAPPINESS

The Three M's
Miracles
Mindfulness
Music

The Three N's
Namaste
Nature
Nutrition

The Three O's
Overthink
Overanalyze
Overcomplicate
(These Three O's lead to a Fourth O, Ohhh no, Overreacting!!! I've been there and done that quite a few times. (LOL)

The Three P's
Present (Live in the moment)
Patient
Positive Perspective

The Three P's
Pray
Peace of mind
Purpose

The Three P's
Perserverance plus
Passion plus
Pride=
Win in the game of life.
The words of the great Dick Vitale, thank you Dickie V! ♥ ♥ ♥

THE 3'S

The Three R's
Relax
Relationships
Resiliency

The Three R's
Responsible
Respect
Reality

The Three S's
Seek God
Serve others
Sense of belonging

The Three T's
Trust
Togetherness
Take-charge

The Three W's
Well-liked
Wholehearted
Willpower

CHAPTER THIRTY-NINE
Morning Prayers

Here's a summary of my daily prayer in the morning:

Sign of the Cross

* Jesus, my Lord and Savior over my life
* Belief, trust, faith, thanks, and love
* Guidance, direction, strength, courage, and knowledge for being a father, husband, school counselor, and author
* Proceeds for the book (Five Charities)
* Making good choices, being my best self
* John 14:6
* The Crucifixion, Resurrection, Ascension (Acts 1:1-11), and Miracles
* Eternal Life
* Two Greatest Commandments
* Count on you in all circumstances
* Bringing honor and glory to God in how I think and feel and in what I say and what I do

CHOOSING TRUE HAPPINESS

- To have a very strong relationship with God, Jesus, and The Holy Spirit
- Today and every day, for as long as possible, to seek God's Face, be connected to His Presence, and to talk to, thank, and trust God
- Affected people and families from the pandemic
- Health and happiness of students and staff
- Health and happiness of my friends and family, especially my wife and daughters
- All to realize, God's Children, One Family
- Everyone to treat each other with love, respect, kindness, and compassion
- Peace, love, and happiness on Earth
- Confessing my sins
- Recite prayers (Our Father, Hail Mary, Glory Be, and Serenity Prayer)
- **Sign of the Cross**

CHAPTER FORTY
Prayers at Night

Here's *a summary* of my daily prayer at night:

Sign of the Cross

* Thanks and love to God for another day and a great life
* Jesus, my Lord and Savior over my life
* Belief, trust, faith, thanks, and love
* Thanks for my health—walking, seeing, hearing, and talking
* Thanks for a healthy family, great wife and daughters, one of the greatest gifts of all
* All sick and suffering people, especially children and elderly in hospitals
* People in Ukraine
* Strength, direction, positive thinking, patience, relaxation, peace, love, and happiness
* Marriage, happy and healthy years
* Military and our military families
* Those less fortunate
* Those no longer with me physically (especially *Nonno* and *Nonna*)

CHOOSING TRUE HAPPINESS

- Confessing my sins
- Recite prayers (Our Father, Hail Mary, Glory Be, and Serenity Prayer)
- **Sign of the Cross**

About the Author

I *grew up as an only child* in Bensonhurst, Brooklyn. I was born on June 18, 1973. I arrived into this world two months earlier than expected. I was trouble right from the beginning (LOL). I had to stay in the hospital for five weeks. I went home on 7/25/73. Currently, I reside in Great Kills, Staten Island.

I attended Regina Pacis elementary school from kindergarten to 8th grade (Class of 1987) and Xaverian High School (Class of 1991). During my childhood, I enjoyed spending time with my friends and tight-knit family. I liked bowling, playing basketball, chess, and poker.

I am very proud to be an American, with mostly Italian roots. God Bless America!!! Forza Italia!!! My maternal grandparents (*Nonno* and *Nonna*), my Uncle Steve, and my mother were all born in Baucina, a small town in Sicily that's part of Palermo. I have fond memories of speaking Sicilian and playing cards with *Nonno* and *Nonna*. Other beautiful memories include making homemade wine and sauce, and spending holidays with my *Nonno*, *Nonna*, mother, aunts, uncles, and cousins. No two people on this Earth have had more of a positive impact on my life than my *Nonno* and *Nonna*. Words can't describe what a deep and profound impact they have had on how I think, feel, and act.

When I was around 15, my parents got divorced. I was completely crushed and devastated. This is when my journey with depression began. At the time, I didn't know how to cope with the divorce, so I didn't talk about it and held in my feelings. I tried to go about my business. This was a recipe for disaster. Certain days I slept a lot, didn't eat that much, had difficulty focusing and concentrating, and was unmotivated to do anything. I acted out in high school and barely made it through my BA in Psychology at Brooklyn College. However, I did graduate and become the first person on my mom's side of the family to receive a college degree.

Besides trying to deal with the divorce, I also had to deal with my father's issues: compulsive gambling and drinking. I had a very hard time dealing with his problems, because I took them on as my own, and I loved him so much. I struggled accepting and dealing with his life. In a lot of ways, it felt as if *I* were *his* father, but I was only fifteen. I was deeply hurt, disappointed, and affected by my dad's life. I put him first for many years and tried numerous times to help him. However, you can't help people who don't want to help themselves. My fight with depression started at fifteen and continued to around my early twenties.

A turning point in my life was in 1997, when I started working, for about two years, as a substitute school teacher in the NYC public school system. Since I'd always loved children and was good at math, being a substitute teacher was a good fit. This gave me purpose, direction, and motivation to succeed. It directed me toward completing my first Master's Degree in Elementary Education at Mercy College and becoming a 5th-grade classroom teacher at PS 179 in Brooklyn, where I met my beautiful wife, JoAnn. I went on to earn another Master's Degree, in School Counseling, at Brooklyn College. I taught 13 years in various positions: 5th-Grade Classroom Teacher, Math Cluster, Physical Education Teacher and 6th-Grade Math and Homeroom Teacher. Being a 6th-Grade Math and Homeroom Teacher completed my 13th and final year as a teacher, and it was my first year at my new school, PS/IS 180, The SEEALL Academy. This is where I continued my journey as an educator and was a dean for three years. After that, I became a School Counselor for Grades 6 to 8, which is my current title. Hopefully, I will be retiring from this position.

JoAnn and I were married on July 25, 2004. When we booked the wedding, I wasn't aware of the significance of that date. Two amazing events had

ABOUT THE AUTHOR

transpired on July 25: 1) 31 years ago, on July 25, 1973, is when I came home from the hospital after being born. 2) My Uncle Steve turned 50 years old on the day I got married.

When I got married, I was thirty-one. Before the age of thirty-one, I never had anxiety. Furthermore, I didn't understand anxiety and knew nothing about it. My fight with anxiety was triggered after a big life event, marriage (LOL). My mind and thoughts started working against me and relentlessly questioned, "Why I would get married when I'm only going to end up like my parents—divorced?" It seemed as though my mind went back to a traumatic event in my life—my parents' divorce when I was 15—and was fixated on it. And my thoughts and inner voice couldn't stop questioning why I bothered getting married and fearing that I was going to end up like my parents.

The anxiety continued on and off for about the first 3 years of my marriage. On certain days, it peaked, and my mouth would feel very dry, almost as if a little sand was in my mouth. This gave me terrible bad breath. On these days, my energy was drained, I lost my appetite and had difficulty focusing and concentrating. I lost about 20 to 25 pounds, but in an unhealthy way. I looked sickly. One day, I had to go to the hospital because I was getting sharp pains in my chest. I remember laughing hysterically in the emergency room because a man in the next bed said something that I thought was very funny. Anyway, I was diagnosed with pericarditis. I believe the cause was stress and anxiety. However, I took it one day at a time—and, sometimes, one minute at a time—and never lost hope, help, faith, or my sense of humor. And I never, ever gave up.

I was truly blessed on May 14, 2007 with the birth of my first daughter, Isabella! Becoming a first-time dad filled me with many strong emotions—anxiety, happiness, and love. Being a first-time dad was a difficult adjustment for me. However, I was determined not to make the same mistakes my dad had made, and this was quite an emotional experience. Even though there were some intense ups and downs, I was well on my way to living a truly happy life. Thankfully, my fight with anxiety mostly finished around December 2008.

I was truly blessed again on June 18, 2011, with the birth of my second daughter, Olivia! It was quite amazing because it was also my birthday. It was

CHOOSING TRUE HAPPINESS

the best birthday gift that a person could ever ask for! Once again, I was filled with many strong emotions, however, this time I had experience as a dad. There weren't any more intense ups and downs. I was consistently experiencing the peace and happiness that I'd always desired and had been searching for. I was living the truly happy life that I'd always wanted!

Reflecting upon my experiences with depression and anxiety makes me realize that I wasn't managing my thoughts and emotions properly. I let my thoughts run amok. My thoughts and emotions were working against me. My mind was in charge of me, causing havoc and chaos. My mind was my master, and I was its servant. It took a long time for me to realize that my thoughts and emotions were in charge of me.

I'm grateful that I've experienced depression and anxiety, because it contributed to the writing and creation of this book. Also, it taught me how to manage my thoughts and emotions. Now, most of the time, my thoughts and emotions work for me. I'm in charge of my mind. I try my best to not allow my mind to work against me, even though it tries so hard and is sometimes successful causing off days once in a while. Also, my faith is the strongest that it's ever been, and it seems to keep growing. Now, most of the time, I choose and experience true happiness, which is the life that I always wanted to lead. It's my great hope that you can, too. Even though I get my difficult days, I still consider myself a truly happy person who's very rich and lucky. In this self-help book, I share how I achieved true happiness and beat depression and anxiety. If I can do it, then you can do it, too!

Endnotes

Introduction

(1) https://www.azquotes.com/quote/416317
(2) https://quotepark.com/quotes/862755-aristotle-happiness-is-the-meaning-and-the-purpose-of-life/
(3) https://www.quotes.net/quote/66414
(4) (7 Ways to Find Inner (and Real) Happiness, By Ed and Deb Shapiro) www.huffpost.com
(5) (7 Ways to Find Inner (and Real) Happiness, By Ed and Deb Shapiro) www.huffpost.com
(6) 5 Ways To Find True Happiness By Tina Williamson, November 21, 2013 3:21 AM
(7) (7 Steps To Achieving Your True Happiness, Daily Spiritual Inspiration, Blog.Sivanaspirit.com, By Lisa LeBlanc)
(8) isha.sadhguru.org
(9) https://www.deepakchopra.com
(10) https://jackieamaya.tumblr.com/post/112746107832/amp Source: taylorxswifts-blog

CHOOSING TRUE HAPPINESS

Chapter One
Awareness and Being

(1) https://www.azquotes.com/quote/388199
(2) https://www.azquotes.com/quote/380702
(3) https://www.azquotes.com/quote/714735
(4) https://www.azquotes.com/quote/444179

Chapter Two
Relationships: Make Them Really Special

(1) https://www.azquotes.com/quote/1222810
(2) https://www.azquotes.com/quote/646828
(3) https://www.azquotes.com/quote/867218
(4) https://www.azquotes.com/quote/292149

Chapter Three
Appreciation: Think It, Feel It, and Show It Often

(1) https://www.azquotes.com/quote/21381
(2) https://www.azquotes.com/quote/561072
(3) https://www.azquotes.com/quote/617071
(4) https://www.azquotes.com/quote/362819

Chapter Four
Perspective: Keep It Positive, Please

(1) https://www.azquotes.com/quote/351994
(2) https://www.shutterfly.com/ideas/gratitude-quotes/#
(3) https://www.greatsayings.net/david-niven-sayings/
(4) https://quotefancy.com/quote/26524

ENDNOTES

Chapter Five

Positive Support System: Is One in Place?

(1) https://emilysquotes.com
(2) https://www.azquotes.com/quote/249552
(3) https://www.quotemaster.org/thoughts+position
(4) https://www.brainyquote.com/quotes/shweta_menon_1079085

Chapter Six

I Agree—It's Up to Me. I Am My Own Biggest Project

(1) https://www.azquotes.com/quote/859552
(2) https://www.mentalhelp.net/. blogs/being-presenceitself-enliven-the-quality-of-your-life/. Being Presence Itself—Enliven the Quality of Your Life. Blogs About Inhabiting This Present Moment By Will Joel Friedman, Ph.D.
(3) Being Presence Itself—Enliven the Quality of Your Life. Blogs About Inhabiting This Present Moment By Will Joel Friedman, Ph.D. https://www.mentalhelp.net/blogs/being-presence-itself-enliven-the-quality-of-your-life/
(4) Being Presence Itself—Enliven the Quality of Your Life. Blogs About Inhabiting This Present Moment, by Will Joel Friedman, Ph.D. https://www.mentalhelp.net/blogs/being-presence-itself-enliven-the-quality-ofyour-life/
(5) How Do We Break the Habit of Excessive Thinking? (Video) By Eckhart Tolle. http://www.eckharttollenow.com. Oct 3, 2011. 2010 Eckhart Tolle, Eckhart Teachings, Inc. All Rights Reserved (11:06)
(6) Meditation: Eckhart Tolle. www.wisdom2conference.com. Wisdom 2.0. Mar 2, 2014. The Power of the Present Moment, A Meditation. Eckhart Tolle (36:21)
(7) The Blog 7 Ways to Find Inner (and Real) Happiness, By Ed and Deb Shapiro, Contributor. https://www.huffpost.com/entry/happiness-tips_b_3886677. 09/10/2013, 08:21am EDT|Updated November 10, 2013
(8) 5 Steps to Living Your Dreams. Deepak Chopra™, M.D. November 10, 2012 03:00 PM. https://chopra.com/articles/5-steps-to-living-your-dreams
(9) https://www.innerpeacefellowship.org/freedom-is-being-present/

(10) Five Big Things You Should Give Up to Be Happy. Posted June 6, 2018 by Tina Williamson. In Happiness + Fun + Love. https://www.mindfulmazing.com/5-things-to-give-up-to-find-happiness/

(11) "Awakening to Your Life's Purpose" by Kathy Juline. July 2011, from EckhartTolleTV Website, https://www.eckharttolletv.com. https://www.bibliotecapleyades.net/ciencia3/ciencia_consciousawakening13.htm

(12) Aligning Inner and Outer Purpose by Greta Rossi—Recipes for Wellbeing, May 13, 2020. https://www.tbd.community/en/a/recipes-for-wellbeing-5-steps-to-purpose

(13) Awakening to Your Life's Purpose by Kathy Juline. July 2011, from EckhartTolleTV Website, https://www.eckharttolletv.com. https://www.bibliotecapleyades.net/ciencia3/ciencia_consciousawakening13.htm

(14) Aligning Inner and Outer Purpose by Greta Rossi—Recipes for Wellbeing, May 13, 2020. https://www.tbd.community/en/a/recipes-for-wellbeing-5-steps-to-purpose

(15) Awakening to Your Life's Purpose by Kathy Juline. July 2011, from EckhartTolleTV Website, https://www.eckharttolletv.com. https://www.bibliotecapleyades.net/ciencia3/ciencia_consciousawakening13.htm

(16) Give Your Mind a Rest: Practice Not-Thinking. Mindfully quieting your thinking is restful, calming, and restorative. Posted May 18, 2015, by Toni Bernhard. https://www.psychologytoday.com/us/blog/turning-straw-gold/201505/give-your-mind-rest-practice-not-thinking

(17) isha.sadhguru.org

(18) https://quotesgram.com/eckhart-tolle-quotes-on-acceptance/

(19) https://www.inspiringquotes.us/author/8895-pat-tillman

Chapter Seven

Nutrition: You Are What You Eat

(1) https://www.azquotes.com/quotes/topics/health-food.html

(2) http://nutritionquotes.com/161/water-neglected-nutrient/

(3) https://www.quotes.net/quote/7410

(4) https://www.azquotes.com/quote/406303

ENDNOTES

Chapter Eight

Good Sense of Humor: Just Laugh

(1) https://www.brainyquote.com/quotes/milton_berle_106353
(2) https://www.azquotes.com/quote/396047
(3) https://wiquotes.com/comedy-quote-by-lao-tzu/
(4) https://www.azquotes.com/quote/537246

Chapter Nine

Help Often, and You Shall Receive

(1) isha.sadhguru.org
(2) https://quotefancy.com/quote/1551297
(3) https://www.azquotes.com/quote/1024454
(4) https://www.azquotes.com/quote/348554

Chapter Ten

Exercise Is the Key: Just Do It

(1) https://www.azquotes.com/quote/1062268
(2) http://www.picturequotes.com/carol-welch-quotes
(3) https://www.azquotes.com/quote/892566
(4) https://www.10tipsforhealth.com/10-tips-timeless-quotes-to-a-physical-activity/

Chapter Eleven

Love, Love, Love

(1) https://chooselovemovement.org/media-requests/
(2) The top 10 health benefits of LOVE. Payal banka, Lifemojo.com. A few documented health benefits of love. https://www.rediff.com/getahead/slide-show/slide-show-1-health-the-top-10-health-benefits-of-love/20120207.htm
(3) https://www.azquotes.com/quote/870158

(4) https://www.azquotes.com/quote/1364635
(5) https://www.azquotes.com/quote/667153

Chapter Twelve

Pray Every Day

(1) https://www.azquotes.com/quote/169788
(2) https://www.azquotes.com/quote/486048
(3) https://prayer-coach.com/prayer-quotes-mother-teresa/
(4) https://www.quotemaster.org/seeing+the+good

Chapter Thirteen

Sleep Well and Rejuvenate

(1) https://www.quotes.net/quote/34782
(2) https://quotefancy.com/quote/946977
(3) https://www.quotes.net/quote/12486
(4) http://www.wishafriend.com/goodnight/id/4482/

Chapter Fourteen

Hugs Feel Great

(1) https://www.azquotes.com/quote/1258598
(2) The Shocking Truth Behind Hugs, by: Susanna Newsonen. https://susannanewsonen.com
(3) https://www.wisesayings.com/hugs-quotes/
4) https://motivateus.com/stories/hugs.htm. Copyright© 2012 Bob Stoess. Submitted by Brian G. Jett
(5) https://www.inspirationalquotes4u.com/hugs/

ENDNOTES

Chapter Fifteen

Express Yourself in an Appropriate and Healthy Manner

(1) https://quotefancy.com/quote/1279230
(2) https://www.azquotes.com/quote/506791
(3) https://www.9quotes.com/quote/chris-martin-530769
(4) https://www.quotes.wiki/dont-keep-all-your-feelings-sheltered-expres/

Chapter Sixteen

Attitude Worth Catching?

(1) https://www.brainyquote.com/topics/attitude-quotes
(2) SUCCESS, Why Your Attitude Is Everything, by Keith Harrell. September 22, 2016. https://www.success.com/why-your-attitude-is-everything/
(3) https://www.azquotes.com/quote/101846
(4) https://www.brainyquote.com/topics/attitude-quotes
(5) https://www.azquotes.com/quote/890785

Chapter Seventeen

Dream On

(1) https://www.azquotes.com/quote/518011
(2) https://www.azquotes.com/quote/533537
(3) https://www.azquotes.com/quote/109591
(4) https://www.azquotes.com/quote/300952

Chapter Eighteen

Seek God, and Grow Spiritually

(1) https://www.azquotes.com/quote/690394
(2) https://www.azquotes.com/quote/452421
(3) https://www.azquotes.com/quote/363375

(4) https://ministryofquotes.com/35-quotes-about-god/
(5) https://www.allgreatquotes.com/authors/hailey-baldwin/

Chapter Nineteen

Happy: To Be or Not to Be?

(1) https://www.azquotes.com/quote/827038
(2) http://howtobehappy.guru/step-1-how-to-be-happy-in-7-steps-happiness-is-a-choice-our-choice/
(3) https://www.invajy.com/mother-teresa-quotes
(4) https://bulldogbravebulldogstrong.com
(5) https://quotesgram.com/expect-great-things-quotes/
(6) https://www.brainyquote.com/quotes/adam_vinatieri_1076089
(7) https://www.azquotes.com/quote/1497011
(8) https://www.wisefamousquotes.com/quotes-about-success-no-matter-what/
(9) https://www.entrepreneur.com/article/321404
(10) https://www.quotefancy.com/quote/1734620
(11) isha.sadhguru.org
(12) https://www.azquotes.com/quote/144847
(13) https://www.brainyquote.com/quotes/demar_derozan_933644
(14) https://www.azquotes.com/quote/105828
(15) https://www.azquotes.com/quote/1355402
(16) https://healingbrave.com/blogs/all/quotes-about-helping-others
(17) https://www.brainyquote.com/quotes/derek_jeter_668775
(18) https://www.invajy.com/mother-teresa-quotes
(19) https://www.azquotes.com/quote/968239
(20) https://gracequotes.org/
(21) https://www.azquotes.com/quote/344348
(22) https://www.azquotes.com/quote/859294
(23) https://chrisnorton.org
(24) https://www.azquotes.com/quote/588615
(25) https://www.azquotes.com/quote/532168

ENDNOTES

(26) https://www.brainyquote.com/quotes/derek_jeter_586272
(27) https://www.azquotes.com/author/20186-Milton_S_Hershey
(28) https://www.azquotes.com/quote/1358863
(29) https://www.quotemaster.org/make+a+brand
(30) https://www.azquotes.com/quote/300950

Chapter Thirty-One

What If . . .

isha.sadhguru.org

Chapter Thirty-Three

Acrostic Poem for the PAST

https://www.azquotes.com/author/3188-Harry_Connick_Jr

Chapter Thirty-Four

Acrostic Poem for the FUTURE

(1) isha.sadhguru.org

Chapter Thirty-Five

Acrostic Poem for the PRESENT

(1) https://www.azquotes.com/quote/572226

Chapter Thirty-Six

A theme to live by for each day of the week!

https://www.azquotes.com/quote/823064

CHOOSING TRUE HAPPINESS

Chapter Thirty-Seven

Acrostic Poem for CHOOSE

https://www.azquotes.com/quote/345656

www.ingramcontent.com/pod-product-compliance
Lightning Source LLC
Chambersburg PA
CBHW021057080526
44587CB00010B/282